Mike Rose, a professor in the UCLA Graduate School of Education and Information Studies, is the author of *Lives on the Boundary, The Mind at Work, Possible Lives,* and, most recently, *Back to School.* Among his many awards are a Guggenheim Fellowship, the Grawemeyer Award in Education, and the Commonwealth Club of California Award for Literary Excellence in Nonfiction. He lives in Santa Monica.

Why School?

Reclaiming Education for All of Us

MIKE ROSE

THE NEW PRESS

NEW YORK
LONDON

I developed the essays in *Why School?* from a variety of opinion pieces, commentaries, and blog entries—rewriting, blending and expanding, and updating them in the process. I hold the copyright on this material and want to thank the following publications for printing the earlier work: *The Christian Science Monitor, The Chronicle of Higher Education, Dissent, Education Week, Inside Higher Ed, Los Angeles Times, Sacramento Bee, Pittsburgh Post-Gazette, Teacher Magazine, The Washington Post,* and the 107th Yearbook of the National Society for the Study of Education, *Why Do We Educate? Voices from the Conversation.*

Published in the United States by The New Press,
New York, 2014

Distributed by Perseus Distribution

LIBRARY OF CONGRESS CATALOGING-IN-PUBLICATION DATA

Rose, Mike (Michael Anthony)
Why school? : reclaiming education for all of us / Mike Rose.
p. cm.
Includes bibliographical references.
ISBN 978-1-59558-938-5 (pbk)
ISBN 978-1-62097-004-1 (e-book)
1. Public schools—United States.   2. Education—Aims
and objectives—United States.   3. Democracy and
education—United States.   I. Title.
LA217.2.R723 2009
370.11—dc22   2009011077

The New Press was established in 1990 as a not-for-profit alternative
to the large, commercial publishing houses currently dominating
the book publishing industry. The New Press operates in the
public interest rather than for private gain, and is committed to
publishing, in innovative ways, works of educational, cultural, and
community value that are often deemed insufficiently profitable.

www.thenewpress.com

Composition by dix!

Printed in the United States of America

2   4   6   8   10   9   7   5   3   1

This book is for the students and teachers who populate its pages. Collectively, they provide the reasons we go to school in America.

I also want to honor Bud Reynolds (d. 2006) and Steve Gilbert (d. 2008)—two of the wonderful teachers from *Possible Lives*.

And, as I always do, I acknowledge my parents, Tommy Rose and Rose Meraglio Rose, with me now in memory.

CONTENTS

CONTENTS

WHY SCHOOL? comes from a professional lifetime in classrooms, creating and running educational programs, teaching and researching, writing and thinking about education and human development. It offers a series of appeals for bighearted social policy and an embrace of the ideals of democratic education— from the way we define and structure opportunity to the way we respond to a child adding a column of numbers. Collectively, the chapters provide a bountiful vision of human potential, illustrated through the schoolhouse, the workplace, and the community.

We need such appeals, I think, because we have lost our way.

We live in an anxious age and seek our grounding, our assurances in ways that don't satisfy our longing— that, in fact, make things worse. We've lost hope in the public sphere and grab at market-based and private solutions, which undercut the sharing of obligation and risk and keep us scrambling for individual advantage. Though we pride ourselves as a nation of opportunity and a second chance, our social policies can be terribly ungenerous. As we try to improve our schools, we rush to one-dimensional solutions, to technological and structural "game changers" that all too often lead to new problems. We've narrowed the purpose of schooling to economic competitiveness, our kids becoming economic indicators. And we've reduced our definition of human development and achievement—that miraculous growth of intelligence, sensibility, and the discovery of the world—to a test score.

Historically, national discussions about education have always had a political dimension to them and often have been contentious. But the current debates are so politicized and combative that positions easily get simplified and hardened, and nuance and possible areas of agreement are lost in the fiery polemics. We as a country and, certainly, the children in our schools deserve better. *Why School?* was written in the midst of these debates and to be sure exhibits a point of view, but I hope that the book can contribute in some small way to a different kind of discussion of why we educate in America.

Why School?

Why School?

FOOD WRAPPERS and sheets of newspaper were blowing in the wet wind across the empty campus. It was late in the day, getting dark fast, and every once in a while I'd look outside the library—which was pretty empty too—and imagine the drizzly walk to the car, parked far away.

Anthony was sitting by me, and I was helping him read a flyer on the dangers of cocaine. He wanted to give it to his daughter. Anthony was enrolled in a basic-skills program, one of several special programs at this urban community college. Anthony was in his late thirties, had some degree of brain damage from a childhood injury, worked custodial jobs most of his life. He could barely read or write, but was an informed, articulate guy, listening to FM-radio current-affairs shows while he worked, watching public television at home. He had educated himself through the sources available to him, compensating for the damage done.

The librarian was about to go off shift, so we gathered up our things—Anthony carried a big backpack—and headed past her desk to the exit. The wind pushed back on the door as I pushed forward, and I remember thinking how dreary the place was, dark and cold. At that moment I wanted so much to be home.

Just then a man in a coat and tie came up quickly behind us. "Hey brother," he said to Anthony, "you look good. You lose some weight?" Anthony beamed, said that he had dropped a few pounds and that things were going okay. The guy gave Anthony a cupping slap on the shoulder, then pulled his coat up and walked head down across the campus.

"Who was that?" I asked, ducking with Anthony back inside the entryway to the library. He was one of the deans, Anthony said, but, well, he was once Anthony's parole officer, too. He's seen Anthony come a long way. Anthony pulled on the straps of his backpack, settling the weight more evenly across his shoulders. "I like being here," he said in his soft, clear voice. "I know it can't happen by osmosis. But this is where it's at."

I've thought about this moment off and on for twenty years. I couldn't wait to get home, and Anthony was right at home. Fresh from reading something for his daughter, feeling the clasp on his shoulder of both his past and his future, for Anthony a new life was emerging on the threshold of a chilly night on a deserted campus.

These few minutes remind me of how humbling work with human beings can be. How we'll always miss things. How easily we get distracted—my own memories of cold urban landscapes overwhelming the moment.

But I also hold on to this experience with Anthony for it contains so many lessons about development, about resilience and learning, about the power of hope and a second chance. It reminds us too of the importance of staying close to the ground, of finding out what people are thinking, of trying our best—flawed though it will be—to understand the world as they see it . . . and to be ready to revise our understanding. This often means taking another line of sight on what seems familiar, seeing things in a new light.

And if we linger with Anthony a while longer, either in the doorway or back inside at a library table, we might get the chance to reflect on the basic question of what school is for, the purpose of education. What brought Anthony back to the classroom after all those years? To help his economic prospects, certainly.

Anthony wanted to trade in his mop and pail for decent pay and a few benefits. But we also get a glimpse as to why else he's here. To be able to better guide his daughter. To be more proficient in reading about the events swirling around him—to add reading along with radio and television to his means of examining the world. To create a new life for himself, nurture this emerging sense of who he can become.

For some time now, our national discussion of education has been dominated by a language of test scores and economic competitiveness. To be sure, a major goal of American education is to prepare the young to make a living. But parents send their kids to school for many other reasons as well: intellectual, social, civic, ethical, aesthetic. Historically, these justifications for schooling have held more importance. Not today.

One last thing to consider as we sit with Anthony. The community college he's attending is publicly funded, and the program he's in is supported by a mix of state and federal grants. The community college has been called "the people's college" for the broad-scale access and opportunity it provides. In his college's programs and in its library, Anthony is pursuing an opportunity that had eluded him in the past. But now, "this is where it's at."

The chapters in this book deal with the topics that inform Anthony's story. The purpose of education. The many faces of intelligence, learning, knowledge. The beauty and accountability of working with people. The power of hope. The importance of rich and varied pathways to opportunity. An affirmation of public responsibility and public institutions.

It matters a great deal how we collectively talk about education, for that discussion both reflects and, in turn, affects policy decisions about what gets taught and tested, about funding, about what we expect schooling to contribute to our lives. It matters, as well, how we think about intelligence, how narrowly or broadly we define it. Our beliefs about intelligence affect everything from the way we organize school and work to how we treat each other. And it surely matters how we think about opportunity. Ours is the land of opportunity—that phrase is a core part of our national story. But opportunity is determined by public attitudes and public policy. Yes, in a sense and at times, we make our own opportunity; that self-reliance is another part of our national story. But from large-scale initiatives and programs (the G.I. Bill or Head Start, for example) to the funding for a coach in a local park, opportunity is created through some form of specific and deliberate public action.

For a number of years, I worked in remedial and compensatory programs, and I see them as intimately connected to our ideas about opportunity. In fact, I like to think of such programs as providing a powerful vantage point from which to consider both opportunity and the purpose of education. The same holds for vocational education, now called Career and Technical Education. Voc ed provides a one-hundred-year institutional case study—a complicated one—on the effects of our society's beliefs about intelligence, opportunity, and schooling.

Playing in and out of all the above are our beliefs about public obligation, about what the public should support. We have been living in a time of disenchantment with public institutions and public programs. At least since the Reagan years, there has been a sustained and savvy effort by conservative writers and politicians to redefine social responsibility, to shrink it and redirect it toward the private sector. This book's final chapters affirm a robust notion of the public as embodied in the nation's central democratic institution, the common public school.

We have a strong tendency in our segmented, siloed world to consider separately social topics that should be considered together. We put into place a testing program without thinking ahead to how it might redefine teaching or about the model of mind that's implied in it. We also believe that the testing program alone will correct political and bureaucratic stagnation and compensate for the need for teacher development or for the burdens poor kids bring to school.

Likewise, we restructure the workplace to give frontline workers more responsibility but don't reflect on the beliefs we have about intelligence (in general and theirs in particular) that will either complement or sabotage the restructuring. Our beliefs about intelligence also play into the way we think about and respond to remedial education at the college level or the reform of Career and Technical Education in high school.

The kinds of opportunity we make available are profoundly affected by what we think education is for, by our beliefs about intelligence, and by the way we conceive of public responsibility.

Why School? provides the occasion—within limited space, admittedly—to consider issues like these together in their lived, human context. We're reminded through vignette and story—through accounts of people at work or in school—that beliefs and policies, which can operate at a high level of abstraction and distance, affect life lived daily in the classroom, on the job floor, at the community center. My hope is that the book as a whole melds the kind of general argument of an opinion piece with the more specific details of developing and working in educational and social programs—and the texture and heartbeat of human experience.

———————

Different definitions of opportunity weave throughout current discussions of education, and a deep belief in educational opportunity is a driving force in *Why School?* So I would like to spend some time considering this core American notion.

Opportunity has a deceptively simple dictionary definition. It can be "a combination of circumstances favorable for the purpose, a fit time," or "a good chance or occasion to advance oneself." These definitions seem pretty disembodied to me, devoid of the particulars that compose an opportunity. Except for the rare event—a winning lottery ticket, the surprise departure of someone in a coveted position—circumstances typically don't just combine, don't randomly fall our way. We often work hard to create opportunity, as conservatives are fond of saying, but also—as those on the left underscore—a whole sweep of physical and social characteristics (gender and race, the markings of social class, or disability), economic policies, and social programs open up or close down opportunity. That opportunity emerges from this web of individual and structural factors seems self-evident, but at different times in our cultural history more simplified notions of opportunity dominate political discourse.

Since Ronald Reagan's presidency, the country has been in the grip of the individual-responsibility view of opportunity. Conservative writers and politicians have been skillful in encouraging an ideology of self-reliance and individual effort and in discrediting and dismantling the protections of the welfare state, social programs, and other means of intervening in the social order. Think of Reagan's famous quip that the nine most terrifying words in the English language are "I'm from the government, and I'm here to help." (Sadly, there can be a bitter, self-fulfilling truth to this statement if you strip resources and authority from government agencies and fill them with partisan incompetents—as we saw with FEMA's response to Hurricane Katrina in 2005.)

There is a lot of confusion in our society about the role of individual effort in achievement. As anyone in the helping professions and human services—not to mention any parent—knows, a person's motivation, perseverance, gritting of the teeth are hugely important in achieving a goal. No question. Where the confusion sets in is when we generalize from this fact to an overall model of human development and achievement. This is the individualistic, self-reliant, pull-yourself-up-by-your-bootstraps way of viewing the world. According to this model, it is you alone (though a family's values are sometimes invoked) who are responsible for your success. As a model of development (versus an acknowledgment of a necessary element of achievement), this is nonsense.

No one, *no one*, develops free of local and broader-scale institutions (from a sports clinic to the military), social networks, government projects and programs (from transportation infrastructure to school loans), and so on. And the social class of one's parents—widely acknowledged as a critical predictor of one's own prospects—is, in turn, affected by a whole range of factors (from local economic conditions to tax policy) that are well beyond individual control. Again, it does not diminish the importance of individual commitment and effort also to acknowledge the tremendous role played in achievement by the kind, distribution, and accessibility of institutions, programs, and other resources. And these resources, as everybody knows, are not equally available. Particularly now.

Opportunity is created in a time and place, so let's focus on our time and place. What is the economic and social backdrop of this particular discussion of opportunity? Despite the upheaval of the Great Recession, the United States remains the global economic giant and for some time has posted strong productivity numbers. The rich profited immensely during the past few decades, favored by a whole range of policies and practices, from lax regulation on corporations to tax cuts. The very rich have been making a killing: their income rose 136 percent during the presidency of George W. Bush, and in post-Recession times, their net worth has continued to rise dramatically in concert with the rebounding stock market.

In contrast, the income of much of the sprawling middle class has stagnated, and the value of one of their primary assets, their homes, has plummeted. Their employment security has also been buffeted by corporate restructuring, the influx of new technologies, outsourcing, and more. These people work longer and harder—thus the nation's impressive productivity numbers—but don't see their income increase accordingly.

Those in the working class live a tenuous existence,

vulnerable to layoffs, working in nonunion settings with fragile rights, holding down more than one job. They have no, or minimal, health insurance, and even if the Affordable Care Act can be fully implemented, tens of millions will remain uninsured. They're locked into a working life of low wages, a paycheck or two away from big trouble.

Among the poorest Americans, the threats to sustenance, shelter, and health are continuous, brutal, and increasing. The poverty that Katrina in her fury revealed to the nation exists across the republic, concentrated in cities, spread throughout rural landscapes.

We live in a time of flattened economic mobility. There have been astronomical gains in income and wealth at the top, and chicken-feed increases in income among some in the working class, but for the majority of Americans, the basic driving principle that hard work will yield movement up the ladder of prosperity is not realized. And for a sizable number of people at the lower end of the economy, an already hard life has gotten harder. From 2000 to 2008, at least five million more Americans fell into poverty. By 2010, a shocking 22 percent of children under eighteen were poor. "Income inequality is growing," notes a special report in *The Economist*, "to levels not seen since the Gilded Age." In such an economic and social structure, "a good chance to advance oneself" or "a favorable combination of circumstances" is available to fewer and fewer people, particularly those at the bottom.

Americans have long looked to education as a way to advance themselves. They also see it as the primary means to overcome social class inequalities; Horace Mann called education "the great equalizer" for those born of humble origins. These powerful beliefs lead us to another cultural tangle. Education *is* a means to enhance one's economic prospects. (And it provides a whole lot more in terms of one's own intellectual development.) But education alone is not enough to trump some social barriers like racist hiring practices or inequality in pay based on gender. Furthermore, for disadvantaged populations—particularly the most impoverished—education must be one of a number of programs that would include health care, housing, family assistance, and so on. So, yes, we should create educational opportunity for the poor, but we should also be mindful that for some, educational programs must be part of a broader network of assistance.

One more thing to say about the creation of educational opportunity, especially in the current climate of suspicion about interventions for the poor: the creation of opportunity involves a good deal of thoughtful work on the part of the provider, and, as well, demands significant effort on the part of the recipient. (This was certainly the case with Anthony's program.) Social programs, compensatory interventions, and the like are not, as some conservative writers claim, a giveaway, a soft entry into the meritocracy. If done well, the creation of opportunity in education (and this applies to other domains as well) also requires great effort, even courage from the person seizing the opportunity. Again, I think of Anthony. What that special program or compensatory intervention assures is that one's effort is not just sound and fury, but is directed and assisted toward achievement.

In this regard, I'm especially interested in what opportunity *feels* like. Discussions of opportunity are often abstract—as in ideological debate—or conducted at a broad structural level—as in policy deliberation. But what is the experience of opportunity? Certainly one feels a sense of possibility, of hope. But it is hope made concrete, specific, hope embodied in tools, or practices, or sequences of things to do—pathways to a goal. And all this takes place with people who interact with you in ways that affirm your hope.

I've experienced opportunity in this way, and the experience has profoundly shaped my life. One early and powerful occasion was my senior high school English class taught by an inspired teacher named Jack McFarland. I have described my time with Mr. Mc-Farland elsewhere, but here let me sketch it briefly in accord with the present discussion of opportunity and the purpose of schooling.

After a lackluster high school career, I landed in Mr. McFarland's English class. He had developed a curriculum that was challenging (we read Homer to Hemingway) and sequenced, with each writing assignment building on the other. Expectations were high, but Mr. McFarland prefaced each assignment with instruction that guided us through it, and then provided extensive written feedback on our papers, feedback that could then be applied to the next assignment. All of this led toward proficiency in reading difficult material and skill in writing analytically.

The pedagogical relationship Mr. McFarland developed with his class was crucial: he set a standard but provided assistance in obtaining it. Furthermore, he believed attaining it was possible. His oral and written feedback—though not always easy to take or enact—was a confirmation of ability.

Though I won't claim that everyone in Mr. McFarland's class experienced it as I did, most of us knew that this guy was working like hell to do right by us.

For me, the class took hold, and for a number of reasons: the structure, guidance, and consistent feedback; the relationship with this mentoring adult that began to develop; the emerging desire to improve and to be more competent—both for my satisfaction and to gain his approval; the gradually dawning sense that this work could lead beyond itself, that it made things possible. Mr. McFarland was the first to start talking to me about going to college. I hadn't given college, let alone my future, much thought until then.

Looking back on it all, I realize that McFarland's class, in addition to giving direction to my life at the end of high school, would also affect how I teach, the way I understand opportunity, and my hope for what schooling can achieve. It was a course that provided me an abundance of knowledge and skill, but, too, the deep emotional satisfaction of using my mind.

The chapters in *Why School?* draw from my teaching, from developing programs for underrepresented or underprepared students, and from conducting research on literacy, schooling, and work.

I've been teaching since I was twenty-four: kindergarten to adult literacy programs, and now in a graduate school of education. Teaching is such remarkable work, revealing the sublimity of development, of learning, of the continual human effort toward mastery and the inevitable disappointment that is part and parcel of the process of attaining competence. Through teaching you learn so much about intelligence, will, desire, frustration, foible, anger, resistance—the human drama. Teaching also grounds you, bringing you closer to the daily consequences of policy decisions, organizational norms, broad-scale social ideologies.

One example comes from the work I did tutoring and teaching in (and later developing) college-level academic programs for students whose previous education and life experiences left them less than prepared for the demands of high-level academic reading and writing. Much has been said and written about such students by policy analysts and pundits, but it is rare to hear from the students themselves or from those who work directly with them. Yet that point of view has a lot to teach us about the personal consequences of inequality earlier in the educational pipeline and about what becomes possible intellectually when difficult material is taught in a carefully orchestrated and respectful way. We will meet some of these students shortly.

And there's more that this perspective reveals.

Looking outward and across college life from the line of sight provided by the remedial program, you see the inadequacies of the typical lower-division curriculum and the limitations of the insular manner in which academic disciplines have developed over the last century. Finally, this vantage point intersects in interesting ways with broad questions about the purpose of a college education and the nature of higher education in an open educational system and an open society. Sometimes the view from off to the side is most revealing.

In addition to being in a classroom and developing programs, I have been fortunate to be able to conduct research on teaching and learning, sometimes working with students individually—as was the case with Anthony—sometimes visiting schools and classrooms. The research provided the occasion to meet a broad sweep of people, not just those students and teachers immediately involved in my study. I got to talk to the custodian and the women in the cafeteria, to the principal and district administrators, as well as to parents and other members of the community: youth workers, clerics, local politicians, the folks who owned shops around the school. They all had something to say.

Before, during, and after a research project, I was reading whatever I could to help me better understand the place I was visiting: histories of local politics and economy, race relations and migration. When visiting small towns, I'd find the historical society. And sometimes the school itself held old documents, like the pile of record books I found sitting on the top shelf in the tiny library of a one-room schoolhouse in rural Montana: the teachers' reports dating back to 1894.

And, finally, it's important to note that the study of even a single child can send you quickly back to the library, reading again the research on language development, or children's conceptions of science, or any of a thousand topics that emerge in the moment, revealing your ignorance.

The outline of what I say about the researching of schools also holds true for the studies I've done of work. Knowledge about how we think about learning and problem solving certainly apply, as does a feel for the drive for competence, the need for challenge, the daily frustrations and breakthroughs of working life. Although some of my research involved the applied sciences and health-care professions, most of it was focused on the thinking involved in blue-collar and service work, thinking that goes largely unappreciated, especially in this high-tech era. My interest in blue-collar work has deep roots. I grew up amid mechanics, factory workers, and waitresses, so this kind of work enabled our family to survive and is sensually and emotionally close to me: the smell of food or machine oil on clothing, the burns and scars and exhausted slump into the chair, the sense of stability that steady work can bring.

In studying work, I considered both novices—to get a sense of how skill and knowledge develop—and experts—to observe competence in full bloom. Typically, I would spend time with people while they worked, watching what they did, when possible asking questions about what they were doing (or asking during a break or at day's end), and getting a palpable sense of what it took mentally and physically to do their work. Gaining this sense of the task (and realizing how I'd bungle what they did fluidly) led to further questions and a greater appreciation of the work's demands.

And, as with my studies of education, I read all I could about the work: the development of its tools and techniques, its professional history and how it defined itself, the economic and social forces that shaped it. I also spoke with other experts—carpenters, hairstylists, old-timers from the factory floor—and with scholars in cognitive science, anthropology, and sociology who could further help me understand the mental and interactional processes that made the work possible.

In preparing this book and thinking back over my own work in the classroom and the various studies I've done, I found myself reflecting on the number of people I've taught or tutored over the years—and got to know through the research.

I've spent tens of thousands of hours with other human beings—from five-year-olds, to people in their forties and fifties, to senior citizens in retirement homes—in some way engaging how they think and learn, learning hugely in the process about what impedes or advances the use of the mind. It has been— continues to be—a majestic endeavor. The challenge in the writing is how to bring the cognitive detail and intimacy into public view, how to render it, and how to apply it to broader social and political issues. The public sphere is where the detail belongs, for collecting it is a testament to who we are, a tribute to our intelligence as a people.

I begin by addressing the question of why we educate, of "why school?" With "In Search of a Fresh Language of Schooling," I raise the question in the context of our current public policy and political discourse. In "Finding Our Way: The Experience of Education" I consider the question in the personal terms of my own irregular path through school and the habits of mind the journey helped me develop.

Then I explore two significant forces in current efforts to reform our schools. In "No Child Left Behind, Race to the Top, and the Spirit of Democratic Education," I discuss the move toward high-stakes accountability, particularly as embodied in the federal No Child Left Behind Act and subsequently in the Race to the Top initiative. In "Business Goes to School" I reflect on the intense and accelerating reform efforts coming from the business community. Both corporate philanthropic and federal reform efforts—which not infrequently interweave—have had a powerful effect on the politics, structure, and curriculum of schools . . . and on the way we think and talk about school.

Definitions of and beliefs about intelligence are woven throughout educational and social policy. In "Intelligence in the Workplace and the Schoolhouse," I use examples from blue-collar work and vocational education—two domains freighted with stereotypes about intelligence—to examine our standard assumptions about intellectual ability and to suggest how we might more fruitfully think about thinking in a democratic society.

Drawing again on the worlds of work and education, I shift from the consideration of intelligence to values and character, further topics omnipresent in discussions of young people and schooling. In the vignettes offered in "On Values, Work, and Opportunity," we see ethical, aesthetic, and craft values on rich display when we create the conditions for students to act in principled ways. And in "Being Careful About Character," I explore the renewed interest in character education, affirming the importance of so-called noncognitive skills like self-control, flexibility, and "grit," while underscoring the continued need for rich cognitive instruction and comprehensive antipoverty programs for the children of the poor.

Standards are the criteria we use to judge competence, and the issue of standards is woven in and out of the chapters of *Why School?*. In recent years, the notion of standards has been embedded in policy aimed at school accountability—Common Core State Standards is the most recent example—but in "Reflections on Standards, Teaching, and Learning," I try to remind us of the central role standards, in the term's original meaning, play in teaching and intellectual development.

Questions of standards, teaching, and learning rest at the center of "MOOCs and Other Wonders: Education and High-Tech Utopia." In this chapter, I use the example of the MOOC, or Massive Open Online Course, to consider the ways our era's enchantment with new technologies has affected our thinking about instruction and education—in the case of the MOOC, higher education.

In "Re-mediating Remediation" I offer an alternative perspective on the oft-stigmatized place of remedial courses in college, presenting both a criticism of standard remedial practice and a defense of well-funded and intellectually vibrant programs of remediation in a second-chance society.

With "Soldiers in the Classroom" I open up the discussion of remediation to broader social issues and programs, and do so through the current and pressing case of veterans of the Iraq and Afghanistan conflicts. In this essay, I offer a model for an educational program that, of necessity, meets educational, psychological, and social needs in an integrated and comprehensive way.

In each of the chapters in this book, I keep trying—in different ways with different illustrations—to extend our understanding of education beyond the economistic and technocratic. In "The Inner Life of the Poor," I consider how education can provide a particular kind of opportunity for poor people to gain agency and become actors on a societal stage that generally has placed them at the margin.

"Finding the Public Good Through the Details of Classroom Life" takes us back to the topic of the opening chapters: the purpose of school and the language we use to describe it. Here I continue that discussion but within the larger frame of the public good and the place of public education within it. I try to offer an approach to Jeffersonian principles from the particulars of the classroom, from the school desk outward to the republic.

In the conclusion, "The Journey Back and Forward," I consider some of the key issues that faced the nineteenth-century educator and that we still confront today, issues that we need to answer in a fresh way as we move into this new century.

And in the Afterword, "Writing About School," I offer a dozen tips for writing more effectively about education, from the kindergarten classroom, to the college campus, to the learning that takes place on the factory floor. Such writing has, I think, its own special challenges and pleasures, and I hope these tricks of the trade help readers engage those challenges and experience those pleasures.

ONE

In Search of a Fresh Language of Schooling

WHEN WAS THE LAST TIME you were moved by a high-level speech about education? I don't mean by the personal testimonials we hear at graduations or award ceremonies, but by a policy or political speech. My guess is that it's been quite a while. We seem trapped in a language of schooling that stresses economics, accountability, and compliance. These are important issues, to be sure, but they are not the stuff of personal dreams and democratic aspiration, not a language that inspires.

For a long time now, our public talk about education has been shaped by a concern about economic readiness and competitiveness. There is some mention of the traditional purposes of education—intellectual, civic, and moral development—but not much. The economic motive looms large. "Education, Knowledge, and Skills for the Jobs of the Future" reads the home page for President Obama's Race to the Top education initiative. Policy discussion is also driven, and increasingly so, by various systems of standards and assessments that have consequences for how schools are rated, run, and even financed.

The economic motive has always been a significant factor in the spread of mass education in the United States, and as someone from the working class who has achieved financial mobility through schooling, I am acutely aware of the link between education and economic well-being. Furthermore, there is an argument to be made for combining this economic theme with measurement technique, especially when considering a system of education as vast and complex as ours. To take just one point, it is crucial to have some means to detect the significant numbers of young people who don't do well in school. This was one stated—and important—intention of the federal No Child Left Behind Act.

But what I want to consider is how this economic focus, blended with the technology of large-scale assessment, can restrict our sense of what school ought to be about: the full sweep of growth and development, for both individuals and for a pluralistic democracy. This narrowing of discourse, this pinching of what we talk about when we talk about school, is evident in the public sphere, the national and regional discussions of education, the goals that motivate action. "It's unlike anything in my experience," a veteran education journalist tells me. "Something is always emerging" about tests and testing. In such a policy environment—one that has been with us for over a generation—schooling can devolve to procedures, to measures and outputs that constrain what gets taught, how it's taught, and how we define what it means to be an educated person.

Think of what we don't read and hear.

There's not much public discussion of achievement that includes curiosity, reflectiveness, uncertainty, or a willingness to take a chance, to blunder. And how about accounts of reform that present change as alternately difficult, exhilarating, ambiguous, and promising—and that find reform not in a device, technique, or structure, but in the way we think about teaching and learning? Consider how little we hear about intellect, aesthetics, joy, courage, creativity, civility, understanding. For that matter, think of how rarely we hear of commitment to public education as the center of a free society.

Now, there *is* an economic discussion of schooling that we ought to hear, but except for a few national efforts such as the Economic Policy Institute's "Broader,

Bolder" reform campaign, we rarely do. This would be a discussion that places individual and school failure in the context of joblessness, health-care and housing security, a diminished tax base, economic policy, and the social safety net. This discussion would include acknowledgment of the continuing erosion of what social protections we have had in the United States. It would also include the fact that education budgets are threatened in many states, programs are being cut, and there are huge and growing differences in school expenditures. The wealthiest public schools spend two to three times more on their students than the poorest. And this dramatic difference in institutional resources is compounded by differences in the material resources parents can provide: from private space to computers and reference tools to tutoring and other scholastic remedies and enrichments.

Calculating, writing, solving a problem, or recalling information take place *someplace* with its economics and politics—which can have a profound effect on what goes on in a classroom. Poverty does not necessarily diminish the power of one's mind, but it certainly draws attention to the competing demands of safety and survival: the day-to-day assaults of the neighborhood, just the tense navigation from home to school. The threats to family stability: illness or job loss—

tough for any family—can unmoor a poor household. A student's own health problems, often untreated or inadequately managed, can shrivel a young person's sense of hope and the future.

We need public talk that links education to a more decent, thoughtful, open society. Talk that raises in us as a people the appreciation for deliberation and reflection, or for taking intellectual risks and thinking widely—for the sheer power and pleasure of using our minds, alone or in concert with others. We need a discourse that inspires young people to think gracefully and moves young adults to become teachers and foster such development.

I'm not simply longing for rhetorical flourish here, although a little scholastic uplift would be a welcome thing. Public discourse, heard frequently enough and over time, affects the way we think, vote, and lead our lives. I worry that the dominant vocabulary about schooling limits our shared respect for the extraordinary nature of thinking and learning, and lessens our sense of social obligation. So it becomes possible for us to affirm that the most meaningful evidence of learning is a score on a standardized test, or to reframe the public good in favor of fierce and unequal competition for a particular kind of academic honor. Education is reduced to a cognitive horse race.

In the long run, in the big, common picture, this state of affairs is just not good for us. Not only does our definition of "public" get distorted, but our definition of learning also suffers. One result is that our national discussions of education, our cultural commonplaces about schooling, are pretty much devoid of two themes I think are central to an egalitarian philosophy of education: a robust and nuanced model of intelligence and achievement that affirms the varied richness of human ability, and a foundational commitment to equal opportunity to develop that ability.

These themes, taken together, fuse the cognitive and the civic, ground the civic in specific obligations to the conditions of learning, and connect events in the classroom to a vision of both a knowledgeable and a good society.

TWO

Finding Our Way:
The Experience of Education

A GOOD EDUCATION helps us make sense of the world and find our way in it.

We are driven—as surely as we are driven to survive—to find meaning in our lives, to interpret what befalls us, the events that swirl around us, the people who cross our paths, the objects and rhythms of the natural world. We do this instinctively; it is essential to being human. So we do it with or without education.

But we are getting educated all the time, of course: by family, community, teachers, pals, bullies, and saints. Our education can be as formal as a lesson or as informal as a lesson learned. This chapter focuses on education that happens in the schoolhouse, the college classroom, the apprenticeship. Education that the culture deems important enough to support and organize.

The question "Why go to school?" has been central

to the way I make a living and define myself. And my own coming-of-age—my own journey from hardship to professional security—was made possible by a series of gifted and committed teachers. So I have lived this question about education as well as reflected on it.

We educate for a number of reasons, and people have written about them since the first decades of the republic: to pass on traditions and knowledge, to prepare the young for democratic life, to foster moral and intellectual growth, to enable individual and societal economic prosperity. All are legitimate, and a good education fosters each of them. But I'm interested here in the experience of education when it's done well with the student's well-being in mind. The unfortunate thing is that there is nothing in the standard talk about schooling—and this has been true for decades—that leads us to consider how school is perceived by those who attend it. Yet it is our experience of an institution that determines our attitude toward it, affects what we do with it, the degree to which we integrate it into our lives, into our sense of who we are. We need to pay attention to the experience of going to school.

Because education became such a source of meaning in my own life—saved it really—I've been attuned to the different ways children give expression to the sense that a particular teacher's classroom is a good place for them: "She's teaching us how to do things we couldn't do before." "Math'll take you a long way in life." "This room is something positive." I've heard this kind of thing in shop classes: New tools "will enable me to do new things, and I'm excited." In college classrooms: "She has helped me see things that were always there that I never noticed." In graduate seminars: "I'm learning these habits of mind that are helping me write what I want to write." In literacy and job training programs: "Formal schooling will help me survive in the future." "I admire and respect knowledge, and those that have it are well blessed." "I thank God to be able to seek the dream I want."

Let me bring this home by reflecting on my own time in school, the kinds of things I learned, and the intimate relationship that developed between learning and my orientation to the world.

I've experienced classrooms as both places of flat disconnection and of growth and inspiration, and this mix has proved invaluable as I myself have gone on to teach. I grew up in a poor neighborhood in South-Central Los Angeles; my father was quite ill and my mother kept us afloat by waiting tables. The schools I attended were not so great, and from my elementary grades well into high school I accumulated a spotty academic record and years of hazy disaffection. I was dreamy, unengaged, fearful of things I didn't understand. But I was fortunate. Later in high school and during my first bumpy years at a small college, I met some teachers who had a lasting influence on the direction of my life. My best education came in the humanities and social sciences, but the gist of what I'm going to share could apply to a wide range of pursuits, from music to biology to crafts and trades.

The study of literature broadened my knowledge of the world. Much has been written about how fiction allows you to participate in imagined worlds. That was true for me, especially when I was younger and much in need of imaginative release, but over time the guided study of literature gave me something else as well. It fanned out to and fostered a knowledge of history—intellectual and social history particularly—philosophy, and art. Reading, let's say, European literature of the early twentieth century brought with it the era's social movements, the crisis in philosophy, the jolting color and form of expressionism and cubism. History then led to politics and economics—which, in turn, were given a human face through the novels I was reading. Abstractions about "political trends and economic forces" were embodied in the physical and emotional detail of the French coal mine, the Chicago meatpacking house, the Nebraska prairie.

The study of psychology gave me a way to understand human behavior. If literature provided historical scope and sweep, psychology took me in close to motivation, perception, learning. I'm simplifying a bit here, for literature surely provides rich insight into human behavior. But my point is that psychology provided a system, a vocabulary to think about, for example, the precision as well as the fallibility of memory or the processes by which we organize information from sight and touch. And psychology gave me a set of perspectives with which to look back over my own life, the beliefs I absorbed growing up, the twists and turns of my development.

Both the humanities and social sciences provided a set of tools to think with. Reading and writing are the megatools. Though I was fortunate to learn to read and write in elementary school—read pretty well, write so-so—it wasn't until my reading and writing were put to use in substantial and meaningful ways that they became more powerful, weighty, and developed critical depth. I learned to search for and synthesize information, to systematically analyze it, to develop an argument with it. Learning to argue in a systematic way is quite a complex skill, and the various disciplines I was exposed to provided help here as well. There are the different ways philosophers or statisticians argue a point, how a literary critic draws on selections of text to support a claim, the questions an experimental psychologist raises about someone's research methodology, and so on. These tools of inquiry, debated and developed over time, carry with them principles of implementation, an ethics of practice, a right and wrong way to do things. They provided me with the means to probe the world and to push back on others' interpretation of it.

Reading and writing gave me skills to create with and to act on the world. The endless writing of papers—and the reading that accompanied them—over time, with feedback from teachers, enabled me to develop skill as a writer. This skill was tested in classrooms and seminar rooms: pretty esoteric stuff, like a high school paper on Conrad's use of imagery in *Heart of Darkness*, and a college paper on sociological theories of alienation. But through assignments like these I was learning how to marshal evidence and frame an argument. And I was also becoming more adept at handling a sentence, folding information onto it, making a complex point without losing the reader. These skills played out again and again on different topics and in different settings, leading to the ability to write a research article, a memo advocating a course of action, a newspaper opinion piece, an essay like the present one.

Acquiring and using knowledge brings its own pleasures. It just feels good to know things and to use what you know. And knowledge of something, baseball to mathematics, heightens your appreciation of it. Also, once you develop an interest in a topic, you want to know more. It has been that way with me about a number of things I was introduced to in school—including the topic of learning itself. My first psychology course in learning was based on laboratory studies; subsequent courses in education explored learning in classrooms, closer to the tutoring and teaching I was beginning to do myself. Over time I was guided to related topics: cross-cultural studies of cognition, neuroscience, and "everyday cognition"—the thinking involved in child rearing, cooking, figuring out what's wrong with a faulty lamp. The acquisition of this knowledge began in school and led outward, a divining rod to the pleasures of the invitingly new.

All the foregoing helped me develop a sense of myself as knowledgeable and capable of using what I know. This is a lovely and powerful quality—cognitive, emotional, and existential all in one. It has to do with identity and agency, with how we define ourselves, not only in matters academic but also in the way we interact with others and with institutions. It has to do with how we move through our economic and civic lives. Education gave me the competence and confidence to independently seek out information and make decisions, to advocate for myself and my parents and those I taught, to probe political issues, to resist simple answers to messy social problems, to assume that I could figure things out and act on what I learned. In a sense, this was the best training I could have gotten for vocation and citizenship.

This has been my story, but I've seen the principles in it demonstrated across grades, across the country. Since much of my account emerges from high school and college, let me offer an illustration from a first-grade classroom, this one in inner-city Baltimore.

As we enter the classroom, teacher Stephanie Terry is reading *A House for Hermit Crab* to her students. Hermit crabs inhabit empty mollusk shells, and as they grow, they leave old shells to find bigger ones; in this story a cheery hermit crab searches for a more spacious home. The class has a glass case with five hermit crabs—supplied by Stephanie—and over the year, her students have seen this behavior. The case holds thirteen shells of various sizes, and more than once students noticed that a shell had been abandoned and a new one suddenly animated. As Stephanie reads the book, she pauses and raises broader questions about where the creatures live, and this leads to an eager query from Kenneth about where in nature you'd find hermit crabs. "Well," says Stephanie, "let's see if we can figure that out."

She gets up and brings the case with the hermit crabs to the center of the room, takes them out, and places them on the rug. One scuttles away from the group, another moves in a brief half-circle, three stay put. While this is going on, Stephanie takes two plastic tubs from the cupboard above the sink and fills one with cold water from the tap. "Watch the hermit crabs closely," she says, "while I go to the kitchen. Be ready to tell me what you see." She runs down the hall to get warm water from the women who prepare the children's lunches. Then she places both tubs side by side and asks five students, one by one, to put each of the crabs in the cold water. "What happens?" she asks. "They don't move," says Kenneth. "They stay inside," adds Miko.

Stephanie gives the crabs a bit longer, then asks five other students to transfer the crabs to the second tub.

They do, and within seconds the crabs start to stir. Before long, the crabs are really moving, antennae dipping, legs scratching every which way at the plastic, two of the crabs even crawling over each other. "Okay," says Stephanie. "What happens in the warm water?" An excited chorus: "They're moving." "They're walking all over." "They like it." "They're happy like the crab in the book." "Well," says Stephanie, "What does this suggest about where they like to live?"

That night the students write about the experiment. Many are just learning to write, but Stephanie tells them to write their observations as best they can, and she will help them develop what they write.

The next day they take turns standing before the class and reading their reports. Miko goes first: "I saw the hermit crab walking when it was in the warm water, but when it was in the cold water it was not walking. It likes to live in warm water."

Then Romarise takes the floor, holding his paper way out in his right hand, his left hand in the pocket of his overalls: "(1) I observed two legs in the back of the shell. (2) I observed that some of the crabs changes its shell. (3) When the hermit crabs went into the cold water, they walked slow. (4) When the hermit crabs went into the warm water, they walked faster." One by one, the rest of the students read their observations, halting at times as they try to figure out what they wrote, sometimes losing track and repeating themselves, but, in soft voice or loud, with a quiet sense of assurance or an unsteady eagerness, reporting on the behavior of the hermit crabs that live against the east wall of their classroom.

There's a lot to say about Stephanie Terry's modest but richly stocked classroom and the skillful way she interacts with the children in it; here, I'll focus on the experience of learning that she generates for her class. Through her artful teaching—her resourcefulness and intellectual spontaneity—she creates the opportunity for students to observe closely and record what they see, to form hypotheses, to report publicly on their thinking, to gain the feeling of being knowledgeable.

Schooling like this is a powerful thing to witness. And a powerful thing to go through. Over time, you see, you feel something: it's the experience of democracy itself. The free play of inquiry. The affirmation of human ability. The young person guided to the magnifying lens, the map, the notepad, the book.

THREE

No Child Left Behind, Race to the Top, and the Spirit of Democratic Education

FOR A GENERATION, the way we think and talk about school has been powerfully affected by state and federal accountability systems that rely on standardized tests to determine a district's, a school's, or, more recently, a teacher's educational effectiveness. The outcomes of these tests are consequential—thus, they are called "high stakes"—for a school's funding and management, and the employment of its principal and teachers can be on the line. In some cases, the school itself can be shut down. The two current powerhouse pieces of federal legislation that drive this approach are the No Child Left Behind Act of 2001 (NCLB) and Race to the Top (RTTT), which was part of the American Recovery and Reinvestment Act of 2009— the stimulus bill.

When we look back over the history of social policy, we see how often a particular policy can have unintended consequences. In the immediate push and pull of passing legislation, questions of broader impact and philosophy rarely get asked. With that in mind, it would be good to step back for a moment and consider NCLB and RTTT in broader terms: what kind of education do such reform programs foster? That question resonates with an even more basic one: what kind of education befits a democratic society?

Let me first consider No Child Left Behind and then bring in Race to the Top, for in a number of ways RTTT draws on the techniques and assumptions of NCLB. In fact, some observers have called Race to the Top "NCLB on steroids."

Historically, education has been a state affair, but NCLB is a federal act that requires each state to develop its own testing program in mathematics and English language arts. Federal funding is affected by performance on these tests, and each state must show continual progress on them until 2014, when all students are expected to demonstrate grade-level proficiency. A further bold move is that the states have to report *at the school level* test results along a number of student criteria, including race/ethnicity, income level, English language proficiency, and disability. Continual improvement by these targeted subgroups must occur, or schools will be put on notice and, eventually, sanctioned. Much has been broadcast and written about NCLB, from defense or criticism of its ranking and potential sanctioning of schools, to the considerable procedural and technical difficulties of implementation, to the resistance from parent groups, school districts, and even statehouses to it.

As I write this in mid-2013, NCLB is more than five years overdue for reauthorization (a provision in the bill enables it to continue until formal reauthorization hearings), and we are clearly not headed toward national grade-level proficiency. Seeking relief from NCLB's accountability mechanism, states have petitioned President Obama's Department of Education, and since 2011 the department has been issuing waivers to a number of states, releasing them from compliance with NCLB. In return, however, these states must implement some provisions of Race to the Top. Even if NCLB is not finally reauthorized, the impulses and principles represented by it, and that are embedded in Race to the Top, will be part of educational policy for the foreseeable future.

One undeniable value of NCLB is that it casts a bright light on those underserved populations of students who get lost in averaged measures of performance.

The assumption is that if schools expect more of such students they will achieve—and the tests will measure their achievement. Early on, some civil rights groups supported NCLB because of its focus on poor children and children of color, and some education activists have used the law to lobby, and in some cases sue, for the curricular and financial resources needed to comply with its mandates.

There are aspects of NCLB that are clearly democratic. The assumption that all children can learn and develop. The responsibility of public institutions to their citizenry. The dissatisfaction with business as usual and a belief that institutions can be improved.

What is worth exploring, though, is the degree to which these tenets are invested in an accountability mechanism that might restrict their full realization. A score on a standardized test seems like a straightforward indicator of achievement. The score goes up, goes down, or remains the same. But there are, in fact, a host of procedural and technical problems in developing, administering, scoring, and interpreting such tests. (And there are also concerns about how schools and districts can manipulate them, and, sadly, we are finding out, simply cheat on them.) "In most cases," writes measurement specialist Robert Linn, "the instruments and technology have not been up to the demands placed on them by high-stakes accountability." No wonder, then, that there is a robust debate among testing experts about what, finally, can be deduced from the scores about a student's or a school's achievement. Similar debates surround the currently popular use of "value-added" methods to determine teacher effectiveness; for example, the prestigious, nonpartisan National Academies Board on Testing and Assessment recently expressed concern about such use of value-added methodology.

There is a second, related, issue. Tests embody definitions of knowledge, learning, and teaching. A test that would include, say, the writing of an essay, or a music recital, or the performance of an experiment embodies different notions of cognition and instruction than do the typical tasks on standardized tests: multiple-choice items, matching, fill-ins. I have given both kinds of tests, both have value, but they get at different things, represent knowledge in different ways, might match or be distant from a school's curriculum, can require different methods of teaching. When one kind of test dominates and when the stakes are high, the tests can drive and compress a curriculum—and research shows this is happening. What is tested gains in importance and other subjects fade. Math is hit hard while art and debate are pushed to the margin—if they survive at all.

There is no doubt that NCLB jolted some low-performing schools to evaluate and redirect their inadequate curricula. The result has been improvement on test scores, and this has become a major source of support for NCLB. The key issue is how teachers and administrators accomplish this revision: through a strictly functional and unimaginative curriculum (which, admittedly, might be better than what came before) or through a rich course of study that, as a by-product, affects test scores.

A teacher I know tells this story. In response to the NCLB mandate to focus on all children, this teacher's district issued a page-long checklist on each student to be used in each class the student took. Every teacher was to mark every time he or she assisted a child, asked if the child understands, noted a behavior problem, and so on. This requirement applied to *all* students, *every* class—though principals, in an attempt to keep instruction from collapsing under the regulation, told teachers to pay special attention to their students who were most at risk. The intention here was a good one, but the means by which it was accomplished was so formulaic and cumbersome that it devastated teaching. Care becomes codified, legalistic, lost in reductive compliance. This kind of thing is not unusual today. It can be ridiculed as a thoughtless local response to good legislation, but the pressure to comply is great, and when there are no funds available to mount professional development, or changes in the size and organization of schools, or other means to foster attentive and cognitively rich instruction, then districts—in the context of a high-stakes, under-resourced environment—will resort to all sorts of draconian and, ultimately, counterproductive solutions.

This concern about the nature of a school's response to high-stakes pressure is especially pertinent for those students at the center of most reform efforts: poor children, immigrants, students from non-dominant racial and ethnic groups. You can prep kids for a certain kind of test, get a bump in scores, yet not be providing a very good education. The end result is the replication of a troubling pattern in American schooling: poor kids get an education of skills and routine, a lower-tier education, while students in more affluent districts get a robust course of study.

Now, assessment *is* integral to learning. Good teachers give a wide variety of tests and assignments, make judgments about student work, and probe students' thinking when their answers miss the mark. Standardized tests can well be part of this constellation of assessment, but should not overwhelm it. It's important to remember how far removed standardized tests are from the cognitive give-and-take of the class-room. That's one reason why there is a debate among testing specialists as to whether a test score—which is, finally, a statistical abstraction—is really an accurate measure of learning. Yet the scores on standardized tests have become the gold standard of excellence.

This single-minded focus on testing has, among other things, contributed to some pretty strange ways of thinking about teaching. For the standardized test score to be locked in as the reigning measure of teacher effectiveness, other indicators of competence need to be discounted. One is seniority—which school re-formers believe, not without reason, overly constrains an administrator's hiring decisions. Another is post-baccalaureate degrees and certifications in education, a field many reformers hold in contempt. Fortunately for the reformers, there are studies that do report low correlations between experience (defined as years in the profession) and student test scores. There are also studies that report similarly low correlations be-tween student scores and post-baccalaureate degrees and certifications. These studies lead to an absolute claim heard frequently these days that neither experi-ence nor schooling beyond the bachelor's degree make any difference in teacher effectiveness—and that the test score remains our only legitimate measure of competence.

On the face of it, this is a remarkable assertion. Can you think of any other profession—from hairstyling to firefighting to neurosurgery—where we wouldn't value experience and training? Therefore, we should at least consider the possibility that something is amiss with the studies. The problem is that the studies for the most part deal in simple aggregates and define experience or training in crude ways. Experience is defined as years on the job, and it's no surprise that years alone don't mean much. But if you define experience in one of the ways *Webster's New World College Dictionary* suggests—"activity that includes training, observation of practice, and personal participation and knowledge gained from this"—then you would most likely find a connection between experience and competence. What people *do* with their time on the job is crucial and becomes the foundation of expertise. As for the question about post-baccalaureate work, the same principle applies: What kind of training? Where? What was the curriculum? The quality of supervision? I'll be the first to admit that a number of education programs leave a lot to be desired, but to discount experience and training in blanket fashion is not only wrongheaded but also undercuts attempts to create better working conditions for teachers, more robust professional development, and opportunities for career advancement—all things the reformers say they want.

The qualities of good work—study and experimentation, the accumulation of knowledge, and refinement of skill—are overshadowed by an often inadequately understood language of testing. Experience and inquiry are replaced with a technological metric.

———————

Advocates of NCLB argue that to raise questions about testing is—as former Secretary of Education Margaret Spellings put it—to water down accountability, find loopholes, avoid it. True enough, wily school officials might well hide behind the complexities of testing. Let's be clear: accountability is central to any public institution. But simplified, single-shot accountability mechanisms will yield simplified compliance, and therefore they need to be scrutinized.

NCLB has been driven by a masterful rhetoric that casts dissent from its agenda as "the soft bigotry of low expectations." There can be "no excuses" for the low performance of poor, immigrant, and racial and ethnic minority kids, as measured by the tests NCLB and now RTTT support. I appreciate this "no excuses" stance. Our schools have an unacceptable record with the populations targeted by NCLB, and the way we perceive the ability and potential of these populations, what we expect of them intellectually, is a key element in their achievement. But it is one element, a necessary but not sufficient condition. What is troubling on a public policy level is the way the NCLB rhetoric of "no excuses" shifts attention from economic and social conditions that affect academic achievement. Poverty is a case in point.

What NCLB has exactly right is the assertion that children's cognitive potential is influenced by much more than their income level. But it is likewise naïve or duplicitous to dismiss the devastating effects of poverty on a child's life in school. Yes, there are a number of cases of poor children who achieve mightily. But their stories are never simple, and, as any teacher who follows her students' lives will tell you, their achievement can be derailed by one bad break.

Not too long ago, I was sitting with a veteran teacher from the rural South. We were flipping through her school's yearbook from a decade before. The school has a reputation for doing well by its students, most of whom come from low-income families.

And there page by page were bright faces, testaments to high hopes, young people in plays, on the basketball court, the lists of awards for academics or athletics, the full smile of the student picked for "all-around achievement." Some of these students were successful, finished school, went on to college, an occupational program, or a military career. But some had to quit when parents were laid off or crippled by illness, and they, in turn, got caught in a cycle of low-level jobs. Some girls got pregnant and dropped out. Some boys were lost to the streets. Two were shot. The teacher closed her eyes as she told of seeing one of the boys in the bus station, disheveled and strung out. The rhetoric of "no excuses"—though it has a legitimate point to make—can deflect our attention from the plain, brutal reality of so many young people's lives.

It seems difficult for us as a culture to perceive simultaneously the physical and psychological devastation wrought by poverty *and* the cognitive potential that continues to burn within. We tend either to lighten the effects of economic disruption with appeals to self-help and hard work, or we see only blight and generalize it to intellectual capacity. In an earlier book, I appealed for a binocular vision when regarding poor kids in school, a vision that affords both damage and promise, that enables one to be mindful of the barriers to achievement and still nurture the possible.

————————

Race to the Top shares some of the same goals as NCLB—for example, test-based accountability and eliminating the achievement gap—but within a more comprehensive reform framework that includes one-time funding to implement that agenda. One of the bitter complaints about NCLB is that it is an un-funded mandate. It places a set of high-stakes require-ments on schools without providing the resources to meet those requirements. The defining feature of Race to the Top is that it makes funding available though an elaborate competition. In order to com-pete, states must provide evidence that they fulfill or are on the road to fulfilling the tenets of the Depart-ment of Education's school reform agenda, which include: assessing principal and teacher effectiveness through test-based performance measures, developing standards and means of assessing mastery of them, promoting charter schools, implementing data sys-tems to improve instruction, and turning around low-achieving schools. These criteria are further broken out into subtopics with each carrying so many points, totaling 500. There have been three rounds of competition so far that have resulted in grants to eighteen states and the District of Columbia.

Supporters of Race to the Top—and this would be true for the architects of NCLB—believe that to move a massive and, to their minds, ineffective school system to change, you need big tools. Competition is a big tool indeed, and it fits into the American ethos. The benefits of this competition, both President Obama and Secretary of Education Arne Duncan point out, go beyond the winners, for those states that were not awarded grants had to enact and in some cases change policies to be competitive. So, for example, legislators lifted caps on charter schools or adopted Common Core Standards. As well, some of the funded states have done things that can benefit everyone—such as developing Web-based materials and guidelines for those Common Core Standards. As happens in the free market, RTTT advocates claim, competition destabilizes a rigid system and sparks change and innovation.

Race to the Top is part of an ambitious package of school reform initiatives that also includes a competitive grant to assist in turning around failing schools and an award program to spur innovation in both K–12 and college. As with NCLB, in the language associated with all three initiatives there is an affirmation of young people's potential and of the right to a quality education, with particular concern expressed for the most vulnerable students. In fact, a civil rights discourse infuses Secretary Duncan's speeches on Race to the Top. As with NCLB, there is a commonsense quality to many of the proposals in RTTT and the other two initiatives. Developing better ways to assess the effectiveness of those who teach our kids, turning around failing schools, encouraging innovation—these are reasonable goals with clear societal benefits.

From the beginning, though, there have been concerns about Race to the Top, and as its program of reform has unfolded, these concerns have heightened. Conservatives and liberals alike have worried about the continued reach of the federal government into local school management, personnel, and curricular decisions—a reach given special power through the money involved. Advocates for public education have also been concerned about the possible erosion of state funding and support for public schools, given the policy of encouraging alternative types of schools, such as charter schools, and the nonprofit and for-profit management organizations that administer them. Finally, though the architects of Race to the Top distanced their initiative from the increasingly unpopular NCLB, RTTT shares the same commitment as the earlier program to standardized testing as a central technology of school reform.

As the first Race to the Top competition got underway in late 2009, there was some confusion about the process and the criteria for the award: the scoring rubric listed six categories with nineteen subcategories and seventeen further categories subordinate to the nineteen. Each category was assigned a certain number of points, and the points were weighted. When the winners (Tennessee and Delaware) were announced, a number of analysts with no vested interest in the outcome concluded that the scoring—in spite of all those seemingly precise categories and metrics—was, in fact, puzzling and arbitrary.

While advocates for RTTT tout the benefits of competition, there is a notable downside. To be competitive, states often have to rush through legislation or repeal legislation on the books, all of which intensifies the horse-trading, strong-arm dynamics of school politics—not always a prescription for wise decisions and public benefit. Again, big money is involved for cash-strapped districts, giving that federal reach into local affairs a great deal of power. And a lot of states that go through all this sound and fury come out empty handed, leaving a thick residue of internal conflict and resentment. Civil rights and educational advocacy groups point to another liability. Many states that don't win have significant populations of poor children in their schools, so they lose out on critical resources that would go to them in a needs-based system. As policy scholar Tina Trujillo observes, one-time competitive funding is clearly better than no funding at all, but it does not address the (admittedly difficult) broader issue of systemic inequality in educational resources.

The ultimate test of public policy is how it works on the ground, so let's go to ground zero, to Chicago, the place where Arne Duncan, before he became Secretary of Education, was the CEO of the public schools and where some of the tenets of RTTT were shaped. A friend of mine—let's call her Shirley—has been involved in Chicago education for thirty years and paints a vivid picture of the liabilities of RTTT as it is enacted in the low-income Black and Latino communities where she works. Shirley will be the first to tell you—for it has long been her focus—that there is a lot that needs to change in the way poor kids are educated in Chicago. She knows intimately the intractability of district bureaucracy, the inadequate curriculum, the damage done by teachers who shouldn't be teaching. Illinois was one of the winning states in the third round of RTTT competition, and she welcomes the funding. But she has watched in dismay and disbelief—her voice keeps rising during our conversation—as RTTT has played out around her. The push toward the conversion of regular public schools to charter schools, or the creation of new charters, provides an example.

Shirley's not against charter schools and works with several that she admires. But her description of the general charter scene in her communities matches the national picture: on average, there is not a lot of difference between the outcomes of charter schools and comparable public schools. There are some very good ones, a lot in the middle, and some low-performing ones. And charter schools tend to have significantly fewer special needs students than the public system, in fact, some charters, as a by-product of their rules and regulations and their demand for parental involvement, end up getting students who are more prepared for school.

Yet, although the charter schools in her area of the city are generally on par with the traditional public schools, charters don't get closed, while two public schools are slated for closure, and a third is in "turnaround," a process that could lead to charter conversion or closure. One of the reasons the district closes schools is underenrollment—a rationale Shirley understands—but she cites two instances where the schools slated for closure have records superior to the charter schools in the area. In fact, one of the schools has an enviable record of students' surpassing the district's standards by six percentage points, while the charter right across the street that contributed to this school's underenrollment has markedly lower scores. "People see this," she says pointedly. "They may be poor and lack education, but they're not stupid. Why isn't their successful neighborhood school being supported? They feel bamboozled."

Closing a school and transferring its students is unsettling under the best of circumstances. (Recall a comparable institutional disruption: the outcry from working- and middle-class communities in 2011–2012 when Catholic churches were being shuttered from Boston to Detroit.) For low-income communities, the school is often one of the few remaining institutions. Transfer also brings to the fore issues with transportation, with navigating streets that mark gang turf, with shifting kids from the familiar to the strange. And all this happens in communities already buffeted by uncertainty about employment, housing, health care, and food on the table. Furthermore, and again Shirley's local observations match national research, teachers and principals in the new settings are not necessarily more experienced or permanent than in the old, and sometimes less so. These are challenging assignments, and the turnover is high. So the goal of RTTT, "an equitable distribution of effective teachers and principals," isn't fulfilled. A policy intended to enact a new civil rights of educational opportunity contributes to community instability—the last thing these communities need.

I think that one indication of the value of a piece of social policy is the public conversations it sparks, the issues it gets us to ponder. Civil rights legislation, for example, gave rise to a moral debate in the nation, a self-examination of our history and first principles. NCLB and RTTT do raise important questions about equity and expectation, and this is a major contribution to a democratic discourse about schooling. But unless a testing and accountability program is part of a larger effort that includes educational enrichment and teacher professional development we get, instead, a focus on scores, rankings, and an elaborate technology of calibration and compliance.

Race to the Top also raises broad questions about innovation in public education and makes funding contingent on change. Secretary Duncan has said that he would like to see this approach to federal aid to education become the norm. Innovation in structure and procedure is necessary for any organization—from hospitals to schools to churches—to become more responsive to its constituency. But the model of change has to be built on deep knowledge of how the organization works, its history, its context, its practices. The model of change in Race to the Top seems to be drawn from ideas in the air about modern business, ideas about competition, innovation, quick transformation, and metrics—an amalgam of the economistic and the technocratic. This is not a model of change appropriate for schools, for though schools surely have business components to them—from food service to facilities construction—they are more than a business, and have as their ultimate goal the development of children.

The kinds of schools that primarily concern me here—underperforming schools in poor communities—need fresh thinking, to be sure, but around core ideas that, in some instances, run counter to those in NCLB and RTTT.

Poor schools need stability and shoring up of the resources they do have. They need long-term development of teachers and principals who are familiar with their struggles and committed to the students in their communities. These schools need to be tightly connected to social and health services—for many of their students carry big burdens—having some of those services on the school site, if possible. The schools should become focal institutions in their communities, involving parents and networking with existing community groups and agencies working for educational and economic improvement, becoming a neighborhood meeting place and a center for civic activity. A separate Obama administration initiative called Promise Neighborhoods does award grants to local programs and agencies that provide health and social services—a very good thing. My concern is that the provision of services is conceived as an add-on rather than an organic part of school reform itself, and the services are awarded by competition to only a percentage of the neighborhoods and schools that need them.

In addition to structural and human support (decent class sizes, aides), teachers need extended, substance-rich professional development, and this development can emerge from the faculty itself, identifying their own needs and interventions, as some successful professional development programs allow. And the faculty needs to work with and help create a first-class, wide-ranging curriculum with assessments appropriate to it. All children need rules and regulations and codes of conduct, but need in equal measure a concentrated effort to engage their minds. The kids in poor schools tend to get a lot more of the former than the latter. NCLB and RTTT do not address that imbalance, and, in fact, can intensify it. Particular effort has to be made to develop a strong and consistent curriculum for English language learners and for children with special needs—these are some of the areas where innovation is crucial.

As I noted earlier, elements of NCLB and RTTT are democratic in intent and could lead to democratic ends. Imagine the power of the "no excuses" stance repurposed toward the sketch of school reform I just offered: there can be no excuses for not providing health care for kids, for not supporting the basic needs of their families, for not helping their teachers develop a robust curriculum. Or consider RTTT's belief in innovation and recognition that money matters, and turn that commitment toward creating in poor schools the curriculum and educational enrichment we see in the affluent schools on the other side of town.

At the conclusion of his study of the American welfare state, *The Price of Citizenship*, historian Michael

Katz sums up his concerns about the use of market models to fulfill social obligations: "Market models seem appropriate to us when we deal with strangers— with the alien collectivity rather than the familiar individual." Katz's observation about markets and obligations applies equally to school reform, which, in our time, contains a hefty influence of market ideology. To think of the students Shirley sees daily walking into their Chicago classrooms as individuals, to understand the hardship and promise of their lives and the profound needs of their schools and neighborhoods would be the precondition for creating an effective and truly democratic school reform.

FOUR

Business Goes to School

"THOSE WHO CANNOT REMEMBER the past," observed the great American philosopher George Santayana, "are condemned to repeat it." If Santayana wanted a textbook-perfect illustration of his aphorism, he could find it in both the approach and the rhetoric of contemporary school reform. Come with me back to the future.

In the early decades of the twentieth century, public schools came under severe attack, with magazines such as the *Saturday Evening Post* and *Ladies' Home Journal* leading the way. Schools were assailed as being antiquated and inefficient. "[T]he American public-school system," wrote one critic, "is an absolute and total failure."

This was the era of scientific management and the efficiency expert. Modern business was in ascendance. The nation was abuzz with talk of economizing and making more efficient everything from factory work to running a household to the practice of the ministry. So it was the notion of efficiency that shaped both the direction and language of school reform of the time.

School administrators began to see themselves as "school executives." There was a call from various experts for "'educational engineers' to study this huge business of preparing youth for life." Precise standards and metrics were developed to help teachers determine their efficiency: "Having these definite tasks laid upon her, [the teacher] can know at all times whether she is accomplishing the things expected of her or not." Anyone falling short would be "unmistakably shown to be a weak teacher." There were further suggestions to cut costs by cutting salaries while increasing class size and teaching load. The principles of efficiency were brought to the curriculum itself. An influential superintendent devised a system to calculate the dollar value of different subjects: for example 5.9 pupil-recitations in Greek are of the same value as 23.8 recitations in French. Since Greek recitations are so much more costly than French, "the price must go down, or we shall invest in something else."

I remember being flabbergasted when, as a graduate student, I read all this in historian Raymond Callahan's *Education and the Cult of Efficiency*. Many of these reform

recommendations got pretty absurd—that Greek recitation business gives only a taste—before they col-
lapsed under their own weight. (Though, sadly, the
ethos of administrative pseudoscience would stay
with us for a long time.) But what was sobering was
the fact that many of these efficiency advocates were
leaders in education, high-profile smart people caught
up in what seemed like the best new managerial science of the time. Counting, measuring, quantifying—
no matter how intricate the phenomenon—would
provide the answer to the era's vexing problems.

Once again, there is a powerful and concerted
attempt assisted by mass media to portray public
education as a catastrophic failure. Once again, the
business framework and businesspeople play a huge
role in contemporary school reform—actually, more
so today. Once again, reformers are equipped with
what seems like the best new science—the economist's
way of framing problems, digital technology, cutting-
edge statistical models—and a technocratic language
that sounds precise, definitive, and action oriented.
We will "incentivize," "scale up," "move the needle."
(And in line with current business school buzz, what
we do will be "disruptive" and "transformative.")
Since teachers are—when it comes down to it—the
problem, we are busy devising systems and techniques

to direct them. And we believe we have objective statistical procedures to measure their effectiveness.

This managerial approach to education took another step forward in November 2010, when Secretary of Education Arne Duncan gave a speech at the American Enterprise Institute, "The New Normal: Doing More with Less," in which he encouraged educators to "improve the productivity of our education system." What was remarkable about the speech was that the secretary was not only talking about productivity in administration and maintenance—which makes sense—but productivity inside the classroom as well. In one of many moments of doublespeak, he decried the "century-old, industrial-age factory model of education," while calling for the application of a management science mind-set to teaching and learning.

Industrial conceptions of productivity are spread throughout current educational policy, certainly in high-stakes testing programs. And a number of big cities have adopted CEO models of the superintendency. Also, in one report and press release after another, business advocacy groups have been defining the purpose of schooling in economic terms. Kids go to school to get themselves and the nation ready for the global marketplace, and this rhetoric of job preparation and competition can play into reductive definitions of teaching and learning.

There is a tendency in all of this that is worth exploring, one rooted in the technocratic-managerial ideology that drives both business practice and policy formation of many kinds, from health care to urban planning to agriculture: the devaluing of on-the-ground local and craft knowledge and an elevation of systems thinking, of finding the large economic, social, or organizational levers to pull in order to initiate change. In the case of education, pedagogical wisdom and experiential knowledge of schools are dismissed as a soft or airy distraction. A professor of management tells a class of aspiring principals that the more they know about the particulars of instruction, the less effective they'll be, for that nitty-gritty knowledge will blur their perception of the problem and the application of universal principles of management—as fitting for a hospital or a manufacturing plant as a school.

Though "qualified teachers" are praised in public documents and speeches, teachers are often pegged as the problem. Teaching, or running a school, is characterized as just not being that hard. Classroom knowledge is trivialized, and the field of education in general is bemoaned as bereft of talent. My co-workers and I have heard such talk at various gatherings of business leaders and high-tech entrepreneurs, school reformers, and philanthropists. And these beliefs are hardly private. A recent article in the business magazine *Forbes* listed fifteen major "education disruptors," people who the magazine's editors selected as revolutionizing "the largest, most dysfunctional field of all." To be sure, the fifteen are an impressive lot: computer scientists and tech entrepreneurs, a college president, several charter school and online education leaders. But none of them, as best as I could determine, has any notable experience teaching in K–12 schools. And one certainly gets the sense that at the state and federal levels there is little deep understanding of the intricacies of teaching and learning involved in the formation of education policy.

Now, we all know that there are a lot of mediocre and downright awful teachers out there, and a number of schools and school districts are in desperate need of managerial shake-up and rebuilding. No question: perspectives and procedures from the world of business can be valuable here. But once you've swept clean, what will you put in place? Here is where pedagogical knowledge is essential. The reform superintendent in a district whose story I've been following addressed the terrible problem of dropping out by creating a special school for young people who have failed repeatedly— a continuation school of sorts. Classes are small; there is a good ratio of adults to students; and there's increased counseling. These are good moves. But the curriculum is deadly, a repetition both in person and online of the skills-and-drills approach that these students have encountered for years, and without success.

Teaching and learning are not simply technical and management problems. Reformers need to incorporate rather than disregard the rich wisdom of the classroom, for the history of policy failure is littered with cases where local knowledge and circumstance were ignored.

———————

In some ways, the participation of American business in contemporary school reform is straightforward: to urge the preparation of a skilled workforce. Different segments of the business community have been involved in curriculum reform via blue-ribbon reports, or have fostered ties with schools leading to internships, or have donated money and equipment. Some, like the Gates and Broad foundations, have launched major philanthropic initiatives aimed at creating particular kinds of schools. And some have donated and lobbied for overtly political causes like school vouchers.

Though each of these responses is distinct, they can all be seen—and are framed—as attempts to improve American education and create opportunity for young people. And many of them do. There's nothing inherently wrong with business-school alliances, and a lot in favor of them. Many schools need dollars, materials, and repairs that business can provide. School-business alliances can lead to enriched internships and various kinds of mentoring relationships between promising kids and female and minority employees who could serve as role models. Beleaguered, low-status schools benefit from having the support of powerful community figures.

There are also reasons for skepticism.

Some businesses have a direct financial interest in matters educational. No question, the result has been some very good instructional materials and technological tools, but the moment commerce enters the picture, there is the danger of the profit motive trumping educational goals. The significant involvement of the publishing industry in standardized test creation and scoring is one troubling example. And in other cases—as in the intrusion of advertisements into schools—there is no educational benefit whatsoever. A less obvious reason for concern is the fact that business donations to education are tax deductible, so as policy scholar Janelle Scott points out, considerable tax revenues are diverted from the public fund and toward business-certified causes. These causes might well be laudable ones, but the channeling of revenue affects public policy and yet is not open to public deliberation.

A further, larger, issue is this: in all the public discussions I've heard, the focus of school-business alliances is solely on the problems with the schools and what business can do to help remedy those problems. The discussion never seems to include business's contributions to the conditions that have limited educational achievement.

I remember when this issue crystallized for me. It was early in 1991, and a friend, another teacher, showed me a photograph in the *Los Angeles Times* of financier Michael Milken standing before a blackboard in an inner-city school. He was teaching a math lesson to two African American youngsters. Milken is known now for his admirable philanthropic work in medicine and education, but at the time he was a bundle of contradictions: a financial innovator convicted of securities fraud, reborn after prison as a philanthropist. His visit was part of a "principals for a day" program that brought prominent business leaders into schools, so they could see classroom realities firsthand. Such field trips are common, then as now.

Schools are frequently the site of this brand of photo op for the powerful: a politician reading to kids, a business executive conducting a lesson. What is telling to me is that we don't see this sort of thing with other professions. A presidential candidate tours a hospital, but isn't a "urologist for a day." A philanthropist visits a women's shelter, but doesn't lead a counseling session. As a teacher all my adult life, I can't help but be bothered by the familiar implication that anyone can teach. The symbolism of such events would be more on target if visitors did things in line with their expertise in finance: sat in on a budget meeting, or had to count out and distribute the servings in the free lunch program, or went door-to-door trying to convince fellow citizens to vote for a school bond.

But the real rub for me with Milken's photo op is that in his earlier incarnation, he represented an ongoing, damaging trend in American business that pushes short-term interests over long-term prosperity and the social good. Although clearly not representative of all American business leaders, figures such as Milken bring into stark relief a fundamental contradiction in

American business practice: its mix of boardroom ra-
paciousness and public generosity.

Business must examine this contradiction if it
wants to affect educational reform in any comprehensive way. It is a good thing for business to give money
to the schools, but the schools also need business to
consider broader issues of economy and culture.

To take one point, various elements of the business community lobby, litigate, and proselytize against
tax increases, minimum- or living-wage laws, and a
whole range of policies that would help poor and
working-class families better prepare their children
for school through decent housing, health care, and
educational resources. Just think of what regular eye
exams and proper glasses alone would do for academic
achievement.

Instead, what we have is an erosion of broad-
based economic support and, in its place, a selective
philanthropy—which, I'll be the first to admit, is better than selfish, opulent capitalism. But such generosity is targeted and partial. There has been a dramatic
increase in the involvement of large, private foundations in school reform. And some of this foundation
involvement drives a particular ideology that might
not mesh with the general public good.

If business is to help inner-city schools and schools

in depressed rural and transitional areas, it will have to understand school failure within a socioeconomic context. It will have to ask itself hard questions about the way national economic policies and local business decisions have limited the development of communities, and the effect these policies and decisions have had on schooling. Schools in a number of cities have deteriorated as decisions by major industries have devastated their local economies.

The hope for a better life has traditionally driven achievement in American schools. When children are raised in communities where economic opportunity has dramatically narrowed, where the future is bleak, their perception of and engagement with school will be negatively affected. We must ask whether, for example, donating a slew of computers to a school will make kids see the connection between doing well in the classroom and living a decent life beyond it, when all they feel is helplessness the moment they walk out the schoolhouse door. From what I can see, after surveying the position papers of advocacy groups like the Business Roundtable, the business community, perhaps because some of its members so cherish a Horatio Alger mythology, has not thought deeply about the profound effect economic despair can have on school achievement.

The business community needs to take a hard look as well at its members who are willing to create virtually any product and marketing campaign that will turn a profit and at the negative influence these players exert on entertainment and news media. So many of the commercially driven verbal and imagistic messages that surround our young people work against the development of the very qualities of mind the business community tells the schools it wants the schools to foster. Our new economy, we are told, requires people who are critically reflective and can make careful distinctions; who can troubleshoot and solve problems; who have an interpretative, analytic edge; who are willing to stop and ponder. Yet young people grow up in an economy of glitz and thunder. The ads that shape their needs and interests—and the entertainment produced for them—champion appearance over substance, power over thought.

Such tactics make money in the short run, but what effects do they have on youth culture over time? The relationship of mass culture and individual habits of mind is complex, to be sure. But there is a significant disjunction between the kind of youngster business says it needs from the schools and the kind of youngster one could abstract from a youth culture that is so powerfully influenced by business interests.

If business truly wants to have a positive effect on the education of our children, the discussion must extend beyond the problems with our schools to the economy and culture in which those schools try to do their work. Business-school alliances will not result in fundamental, long-range educational change if the terms of the alliances essentially have the powerful passing judgment and bestowing dollars on beleaguered classrooms. A more complex and self-critical discussion will have to evolve. We'll need more than the one-directional reforms symbolized by a billionaire standing before a blackboard.

FIVE

Intelligence in the Workplace and the Schoolhouse

WE LIVE IN A TIME of much talk about intelligence. Yet we operate with a fairly restricted notion of what that term means, one identified with the verbal and quantitative measures of the schoolhouse and the IQ test. As the culture of testing we live in helps define achievement and the goals of schooling, it also has an effect on the way we think about ability. And even though scholars like Howard Gardner and Robert Sternberg have helped us broaden our understanding of intelligence with concepts such as multiple intelligences and practical intelligence, we tend to undervalue, or miss entirely, the many displays of what the mind does every day, all the time, right under our noses.

I would like to reflect on this issue of intelligence anew by considering together the schoolhouse and the workplace. We spend much of our young lives in school, and a much longer stretch of our adult lives at work. And the two are intimately connected in that a primary justification for schooling is to secure a place in the economy. As I've been arguing, this justification is intense today. Furthermore, the schools one attends and the work one does are powerful social markers, perhaps the most powerful, by which we make judgments about a person's intelligence. All of this plays through the aforementioned web of attitudes about formal schooling.

I recently finished a long study of the thought it takes to do blue-collar and service work, welding to waitressing, and it has left me not only with a heightened respect for the intellectual content of such work, but also with a concern about the way we tend to judge people's intelligence by the work they do, and with what I hope is a better understanding of the nature of intelligence itself. Consider how many distinctions we readily make about work that carry with them weighty implications about both the work and the worker. These distinctions are usually expressed as opposites: brain vs. hand, mental vs. manual, intellectual vs. practical, pure vs. applied, neck up vs. neck down. All this is intensified in our high-tech era, and, to be sure, high technology and "symbolic analysis" typically involve advanced formal education and require significant levels of analytic skill. What is worth noting is the way we celebrate the play of mind in such work but diminish, even erase, it in other kinds of work, physical and service work particularly. In our schools and industries as well as in our informal talk, we tend to label entire categories of work and the people associated with them in ways that overgeneralize, erase cognitive variability, and diminish whole traditions of human activity.

We have been hearing for some time now that we live in a new economic age, one radically different from the Industrial Age of just a few decades ago. Ours is an economy built on information and high technology and requires a new kind of worker: creative, problem solving, skilled in collaboration and communication. A smart worker for the smart machine. But work of the Industrial Age, as the authors of one of the many books on the subject put it, "required a contribution of employees' hands alone."

Though there is certainly debate among economists about the nature and extent of this so-called revolution in the economy, the rhetoric of old work vs. new work is very much with us, and shapes both economic and educational policy—and with it our notions about what it means to be smart in the work-place and the schoolhouse.

The trouble is that this kind of talk is inaccurate in its portrayal of so many kinds of work. Most charac-terizations of the new information economy and the new knowledge worker ignore the rich knowledge base of traditional labor. This way of describing the work of the last century masks the considerable brainpower that made it possible. Of equal concern is that such descriptions blind us to the mental resources found in everyday work—this at a time when business leaders are calling to maximize the cognitive content of work and the intellectual potential of workers.

While there certainly are things about the eco-nomic developments of the last few decades that present new challenges and opportunities—the re-structuring of some industries, the degree of glo-balization, the increasing presence of electronic technologies—the commonplace distinction between "new knowledge age" vs. "old industrial age" misleads on a number of levels.

The problem starts with the penchant that many writers on the new economy have for either/or lists. The very distinction between "industrial" vs. "knowl-edge" work is one such binary. Another is the sepa-ration of "hand work" and "brain work," as though

work of the hand were mindless. Yet another dichotomy is that industrial work calls for strictly rote
performance while new work requires learning and
problem solving; so too the characterization of industrial work as "individual" vs. the "relational" collab-
orative nature of new work. The list goes on.

The authors of such lists are trying to get at some
of the qualities of the emerging work of our time, but
what they're describing is a matter of degree, not the
polar-opposite sea change that the lists suggest. As a
reading of reports written during previous economic
eras reveals, each generation heralds the unprecedented
nature of its work: the technological breakthroughs,
the intellectual demands, the transforming effects on
workers. It seems to be part of the rhetoric of our
economic development to describe ourselves as always
on the cognitive cutting edge, the radically new.

But the historical record is more layered and nuanced. Consider technology. New technologies—
from power tools to electronic communication—do
have profound impact on work, but they get embedded in existing work cultures while transforming them,
and aspects of old practice carry over and morph into
the new.

The "new economy" lists also suggest that blue-
collar and service workers don't rely on a body of

knowledge to do their work, nor learn and solve problems, nor have to coordinate and negotiate with other workers. The lists imply that work involving the hand doesn't considerably involve the brain. But when you get in close to the work itself, such distinctions fall apart.

Studies of the factory floor demonstrate that frontline workers develop skill at performing their routines. They learn to work smart, to maximize energy and efficiency. They come to know the properties of the materials they work with and the quirks of the machinery they operate. The foreman who supervises the assembly line is the consummate multitasker, facing some new demand every minute or two: supplying tools and materials, demonstrating procedures, handling personnel frictions, and anticipating problems on the line.

Moving from the factory to other "old economy" manual work, the picture gets more textured. Mechanics, machinists, and all the construction tradespersons continually blend hand and brain. They develop rich knowledge of materials, tools, and processes. They regularly troubleshoot and solve problems. And each trade affords the opportunity to learn and keep learning and to develop specialized competencies. Take, for example, the carpenter who uses a number of mathematical concepts—symmetry, proportion, congruence, the properties of angles—and develops the ability to visualize these concepts while building a cabinet, a flight of stairs, a pitched roof.

Consider this carpenter I observed, installing a set of sliding French doors into a constrained wall space. At one point he stood back, chin in hand, and surveyed the frame, his eyes moving over it, occasionally nodding his head and saying something under his breath. When I asked him what he was doing, he said he was "picturing the door in my mind." He was imagining the pieces as he will assemble them, thinking how the threshold will have to angle down, so that the rain will run off it, and picturing the sliding panels moving across the stationary ones, and where problems might develop with that. As well, he was imagining the look of the casings that came with the door, and realizing that they're too big, given the other woodwork in the room, and trying to visualize alternative casings he could fashion.

The carpenter is performing a number of mostly visual operations on his knowledge of door assembly. He is examining and combining elements of the assembly, moving them, comparing, substituting, or transforming them. And there are not only structural and mechanical goals driving these operations, but aesthetic ones as well—the look of the casings. He is assembling the structure in his mind's eye, and is also reflecting on it.

Writers on the new economy include service work in their discussions of the new work order, though it is typically high-tech, health care, or sales in restructured industries. The classier kind of service. But old-fashioned, commonplace service workers exhibit many "new economy" abilities as well. Take, for example, the waitress and the hairstylist.

In the busy restaurant, the waitress has to remember orders and monitor them, attend to a dynamic environment, prioritize tasks and manage the flow of work, make decisions on the fly. This fast thinking is taking place in an emotional field. Is the manager in a good mood? Did the cook wake up on the wrong side of the bed? If so, how can the waitress make an extra request or return an order diplomatically? And then, of course, there are the customers. Customers enter a restaurant with all sorts of needs, from the physiological—and the emotions that accompany hunger—to a desire for public intimacy. The waitress's tip is dependent on how well she responds to these needs. So she gets good at reading social cues and managing feelings, both the customers' and her own.

The hairstylist's practice is a mix of technique, knowledge about the biology of hair, aesthetic judgment, and communication skill. Stylists get good at converting a vague request ("Give me something light and summery") into a specific cut. They are called on to figure out the source of a problem with a previous cut or procedure and solve it. They are thinking ahead as they work. Listen to this stylist describe what goes on in her mind:

> You've got to add up all these pieces to the puzzle, and then at the end you've got to come up with a thought, OK, it's gotta be this length, it's gotta be layered here, it's got to be textured there, it can have a fringe, it can't have a fringe, you know, so the thought process goes. . . . It's not like we just start cutting. By the time I take my client to the shampoo bowl, after the consultation, I already have a little road map as to how I'm going to cut this haircut.

Instead of this intellectual richness, we have developed a language that falsely defines entire economic eras and entire categories of workers by body and hand alone.

One of the most unfortunate of the cognitive dichotomies I've been discussing, particularly in the lives of young people, has been the distinction between the academic and the vocational. This distinction characterized the high school curriculum for much of the past century and has defined entire courses of study. Though it has been the focus of significant reform over the past two decades, vocational education—and, more generally, the divide between the academic and the vocational curriculum—has been one of the most long-standing and visible institutional manifestations of our culture's beliefs about hand and brain, mind and work.

It is the academic curriculum, not the vocational, that has gotten identified as the place where intelligence is manifest. Such separation plays out on the ground, in the way school people talk, in the formal and informal terms and categories they use. Thus a language of abstraction, smarts, big ideas surrounds the academic course of study, which is symbolically, structurally, and often geographically on the other side of the campus from the domain of the manual, the concrete, the practical, the gritty.

The reforms aimed at bridging the academic-vocational divide—many spurred by federal legislation—have led to a range of solutions. Yet, any reform movement produces widely varied results. Many efforts are little more than minor adjustments to the status quo. But some efforts are ambitious, involving a cross section of a school's faculty over many months in developing a curriculum that integrates academic and vocational material. And in a few cases, a visionary faculty use voc ed (or, as it's now called, career and technical education) reform as the occasion to reimagine the very structure of high school itself and with it the academic-vocational divide.

Unfortunately, such innovation is rare. Intellectual enrichment, when it occurs, is typically achieved by beefing up the vocational side of things with traditional academic content and courses. As a practical matter, this makes sense; one of the goals of the reforms is to render more students eligible for college, so they need to have the prerequisite academic courses. But conceptually, such practice doesn't move us much beyond the narrow definitions of knowledge that separate hand from brain. These biases about mind and work—which have so influenced schooling—are infrequently raised in reform deliberations. Thus, as the education scholar Theodore Lewis points out, vocational knowledge is not perceived as valid school knowledge. This bias will continue to limit a creative rethinking of the academic-vocational divide.

These reductive and limiting ways of thinking about intelligence also affect job training and the way work is organized, even in a time when some industries are trying to restructure and give more responsibility to frontline workers. Consider the following example, provided by the literacy researcher Glynda Hull and her associates. Their research team spent several years investigating the production of computer circuit boards in a high-tech workplace in California's Silicon Valley. What they found was that although the frontline assemblers were expected to be literate and analytical, the managerial structure of the factory and assumptions by managers about the mental capacity of the (mostly immigrant) assemblers contributed to a restricted development of literacy skill among the workers. They were organizationally limited to basic tasks like reading labels; there was little incentive to use or further develop their ability to read and write. Professor Hull's cautionary tale reminds us that even at a time of much talk about occupational change—and on the part of some, a real desire for it—there remain in effect powerful beliefs about mind and work that sabotage reform and constrain human potential.

Economic and educational opportunity is typically defined in terms of slots, positions, openings, or, more generally, by the absence of structural barriers to advancement. Such definitions have been used by the courts to force opportunity where little opportunity existed. But there is another dimension to opportunity, not as obvious, less verifiable, but exceedingly important. As we just saw, it has to do with beliefs about intelligence.

I am not diminishing the kinds of ability that have increasingly formed the core of our century's conception of intelligence, for they clearly enable extraordinary achievement. Rather, I want us to consider other spaces in the picture of human cognition and the effect our partial perception has on the way we think about mind, school, and work.

———————

How should we think about intelligence, particularly in a democratic society? Whatever the basic neurochemical mechanisms of cognition are, most psychologists would agree that the way intelligence is defined and manifested is culture-bound, affected by historical and social circumstances. So it becomes a legitimate act for a culture to ponder its ideas about intelligence: what do our ideas enable or restrict in education, in the economy, in social life? And how do our ideas map onto our foundational beliefs about the person?

As an ideal, democracy assumes the capacity of the common person to learn, to think independently, to decide thoughtfully. The emergence of this belief marks a key juncture in Western political philosophy, and such belief is central to the way we in the United States, during our best moments, define ourselves as citizens. Our major philosophical and educational thinkers—Jefferson, Horace Mann, and John Dewey—have affirmed this potential among us.

The models and language we use have social consequences, a point worth pondering at this historic moment, as we undergo transformations in the workplace, as we struggle to provide a quality education for all. Of course, matters of the economy and of education are affected by a number of forces, but the beliefs we carry about people figure into both the development and implementation of policy. If we believe common work to be mindless, that belief will affect the work we create in the future. If we don't appreciate, if we in some way constrict, the full range of everyday cognition, then we will develop limited educational programs and fail to make fresh and meaningful instructional connections among disparate kinds of skill and knowledge. If we think that whole categories of people—identified by class, by occupation—are not that bright, then we reinforce social separations and cripple our ability to talk across our current cultural divides.

To affirm our capacity as a people is not to deny the obvious variability among us. Nor is it to retreat to some softhearted notion of mind. We mistake narrowness for rigor, but actually we are not rigorous enough. To acknowledge our collective capacity is to take the concept of variability seriously. Not as a neat binary distinction or as slots along a simplified cognitive continuum, but as a bountiful and layered field, where many processes and domains of knowledge interact. Such a model demands more, not less, from those of us who teach, or who organize work, or who develop social policy. To affirm this conception of mind and work is to be vigilant for the intelligence not only in the boardroom but on the shop floor; in the laboratory and alongside the house frame; in the workshop and in the classroom. This is a model of mind that befits the democratic imagination.

SIX

On Values, Work, and Opportunity

BEFORE LEAVING THE INTERTWINED ISSUES of work, school, and ability, I want to address one further thing that emerged from my studies of work and cognition: the issue of values. For some time now, there has been a troubled national conversation about the skills and values of young people entering the workforce, concerns about their literacy, numeracy, and problem-solving ability, and, as well, their weaknesses in the so-called soft job skills: punctuality, responsibility, a sense of workmanship. More recently, with the shock of gang violence and schoolyard murders, a broader and more anguished conversation about youth and values has consumed us. Young people mystify and frighten us; they're opaque, alienated, asocial.

I wonder, though, if our collective anxiety is distracting us from, even blinding us to, a wide range of behaviors and values that are constructive, engaged, and laudable and, in fact, are dearly sought in our national assays of young people's lives. We don't look in the right places—which are, not infrequently, right before us—and more often than not we ask the wrong questions.

My studies of work have sparked some different questions. My observations of young people building a cabinet or repairing a faulty circuit have revealed complex thought and skill. And these observations have also revealed a range of values that would offer an unexpected contribution to our national lamentation over the loss of values.

Let me offer some examples, ones drawn from high school classes in carpentry, auto mechanics, and plumbing—places that might not be, for some, the first places in the curriculum to look.

During my visits, I heard continual expression of (and saw material evidence to support) a desire to do a job correctly, to make something work. We can call the values expressed here utilitarian values, ones dealing with function and use.

Willie is a member of a team that is building computer tables for the district office, and he is showing me the base of one of them. The base is an octagonal oak structure with supports radiating out at four points. The top will be fastened onto these supports.

Willie explains how their teacher helped them draw plans for the multiangled structure, and how they built a prototype first. "It has to be just right," he observes, "or it won't work."

Consider, as well, Nancy, who, with another student, is replacing the brake pads on her sister's car. She works through the class period and into lunch. As she is finishing up, tightening wheel nuts with a pneumatic wrench, she talks about the importance of good brakes, how she is "really picky about brakes," how they can make the crucial difference in protecting both life and property.

And there is Carlos, one of a crew of students volunteering at a Habitat for Humanity site. He is assembling the frames for the walls of one of the bedrooms. These frames consist of two long, horizontal two-by-four boards with six shorter two-by-fours, called studs, nailed vertically in place sixteen inches apart. Carlos begins by measuring and marking the sixteen-inch increments on the horizontal boards, and then lays out the vertical studs accordingly. He measures again. Then he begins nailing the studs in place, driving one nail, then another, stopping occasionally to check with his eye or framing square the trueness of the frame. I ask Carlos about this precision. He says that when the frame is finished, "I know it's going to be straight and well done." He pauses and adds: "That's the way I am."

These young people are meticulous about the work they do, aware of the consequences of error, exhibiting both pride in and commitment to doing a good job. There are ethical ramifications here—Nancy links her work to the safety of others—and a process of self-definition. Carlos's precision is associated with his sense of who he is.

In addition to values related to use and function, I saw ample evidence of values that are more aligned with craft and aesthetics. Christian is completing a bookcase for his room, showing me a small flaw along the base. Under a strip of oak that both decorates and reinforces the base—in a place that no one will be able to see once the bookcase is upright—Christian points to a tiny gap in the otherwise flawless seam where strip and base join together. The gap is between one-sixteenth and one-thirty-second of an inch wide. Wood inevitably warps, and, as Christian explains it, he placed his finishing nails "too high on the strip," thus not correcting for a small irregularity in the oak strip. Next time, he notes, he'll place the nails lower, checking the seam more carefully. Now, though, he's going to fill the gap with putty and sand it. "No one can see it," he says, "but I want it to be right."

I heard comments like this frequently. Students would go over something one more time, redo it, or repair it to make it more appealing to the touch or the eye. The tiny gap in the seam will not affect function in any way, but it violates Christian's sense of what good work should look like—even when the only gaze on it is his.

What has been evident in these examples is the way these students' values about utility and craft direct their behavior. Let me provide one last example that nicely illustrates this point. Peter is working with Sam, a retired plumber volunteering his time, on the sinks in a women's shelter. Peter works hard and fast, taking stairs two at a time, says he enjoys getting this experience with a seasoned plumber, and is curious about the function of things—he'll ask Sam to repeat a task or manipulate a device so he can see how it works. At this moment, they're replacing the faucets on a bathroom sink and are about to fit the sink back into its cabinet. Peter takes a quick look at the drainpipe and P-trap, running his finger inside the trap. "Oh, look at this!" he says to Sam. The trap is corroded, and if you squat down, you can see the buildup of rust and debris. "We've gotta change this," he says, "we can't put it back together like this."

The schedule for the day specified faucets only, so Peter goes in search of his instructor, wanting to get approval for a new P-trap that he will then have to go find in the crew's supplies. Peter's curiosity, his thoroughness, and his desire to do good work combine here toward action that was unplanned and that both satisfies his sense of workmanship and yields benefit to others.

These illustrations reveal some of the very qualities whose loss we bemoan: They also generate for me some thoughts on a number of issues related to education, work, values, and opportunity.

The first has to do with our ways of seeing. The constructing and repairing events described here are, in some ways, pretty mundane, not as sensational as the usual glimpses we get of young people. To be sure, these events are part of a flow of experience that also can include isolation, peer insult, commodified romance, distorted masculinity, and both virtual and real violence. We're right to worry about this—especially since adults are ultimately responsible for more than a little of it. But young people's lives are complex and nuanced. What might come into focus if we got in close to other activities that mattered to them? I presented examples drawn from a particular kind of work, but, in my experience, we could find similar moments in a writing class or chemistry lab, in church projects, farm routines, or a martial-arts program. If all we look for is pathology, we'll miss everyday moments of promise.

These vignettes are also reminders of something we easily forget, particularly in times of distress. The development of values occurs best in situations where young people are engaged in ongoing, meaningful activity. The values displayed in these examples were not taught in a didactic way, nor were they the topic of a lecture or instilled through lists, logos, or dis-embodied religious texts. They emerged from engagement in substantial work. They were not laid on from above.

The final point, and for me the critical one, has to do with the opportunity we as a society provide for young people to become engaged in sustained activity that requires hand and brain, action, and reflection on that action. It costs money to do this. It calls for careful planning. And it requires the involvement of committed, skillful adults. Peter's moment with that P-trap—the exercise of his curiosity, knowledge, and workmanship—was made possible by the negotiations his instructor had with the agencies that ran the women's shelter, by the presence of the older, volunteer plumber, and by all the training Peter's instructor had provided before that day in the field. This means a commitment to young people's development over the long haul.

The question we should be asking is not: what has happened to our young people? Rather, we should think hard about the kind and number of opportunities we provide for them to develop and exhibit behavior and values that have personal and social benefit.

SEVEN

Being Careful About Character

ONE OF THE SUREST CLAIMS one could make about how to lead a successful life, in or out of school, is that qualities such as determination, perseverance, self-control, and a degree of flexibility matter a lot. In American education, these qualities often get labeled as "character," and there is a rapidly growing interest in how to teach and measure it. Conferences, consultants, and special issues of journals are focusing on character, and in late 2012 journalist Paul Tough wrote a bestselling book, *How Children Succeed*, that nicely summarizes the various bodies of research and advocates behind the current boom.

As I watch twenty-first-century character education take off, I worry about two things, my worry born out of decades of watching new ideas—or, often, old wine in new bottles—capture our attention. One concern has to do with the way these qualities of character get defined, the other with the focus of a fair amount of the discussion on the education of low-income children.

———————

There is some confusion as to what to call qualities like perseverance or self-control. Some refer to them as personality traits, which in psychology refers to a set of relatively stable characteristics. Yet a quality like perseverance might change with setting, age, and task. I am dogged in writing an essay like this but become pretty squirrelly with tax forms or figuring out electronic devices.

A further, and I think major, problem with terminology and definition has to do with the widespread tendency to refer to these qualities as "noncognitive" traits or skills. To understand the problem here, consider the definition of cognition and the way it's been distorted in our recent educational history.

Cognition traditionally refers to a wide and rich range of mental processes, from memory and attention, to comprehending and using language, to solving a difficult problem in physics or choreography or sharing an office with someone. But over the last few decades cognition has been reduced to a shadow of its former self. Under No Child Left Behind and Race to the Top, cognition in education policy has increasingly come to be defined by the skills measured by standardized tests of reading and mathematics. And as economists have gotten more involved in education, they've needed quantitative measures of cognitive ability and academic achievement for their analytical models, so they've used IQ or other standardized test scores (like the Armed Forces Qualification Test or AFQT) as a proxy for intelligence or achievement. From the Latin *cognoscere*, to come to know, or *cogito ergo sum*, I think therefore I am, we've devolved to a few digits on the AFQT.

Many of those who advocate character education believe that our nation's educational focus on cognition has been misguided. Rather than focusing our energies on the academic curriculum—or on academic intervention programs for the poor—we need to turn our attention to the development of qualities of character, for as much or more than cognition, it is these qualities that account for success in school and life.

It is healthy to be reminded about the fuller scope of education in our test- and grade-obsessed culture, but what concerns me is that the advocates for character accept without question the reductive notion of cognition that runs through our education policies, and by accepting it, further affirm it. The problem is exacerbated by the aforementioned way economists carve up and define mental activity. If cognition is represented by scores on ability or achievement tests, then anything not captured in those scores—like the desired qualities of character—is, de facto, noncognitive. We're now left with a skimpy notion of cognition and a reductive dichotomy to boot. This downplaying of the cognitive and the construction of the cognitive/ noncognitive binary will have some troubling implications for education, especially for the education of the children of the poor.

To begin with, the labeling of character qualities as "noncognitive" misrepresents them—particularly if you use the truer, richer notion of cognition. Self-monitoring, for example, has to involve a consideration and analysis of one's performance and mental state—a profoundly cognitive activity. Flexibility demands a weighing of options and decision making. This is not just a problem of terminology, for if you don't have an accurate description of something, how can you help people develop it?

Furthermore, these desired qualities are developed over time in settings and relationships that are meaningful to the participants, which most likely means that the settings and relationships will have significant cognitive content. Two of the classic preschool programs that have provided a research base for the character advocates—the Perry Preschool and Abece-darian Projects—were cognitively rich in imaginative play, language use, and activities that required thought and cooperation.

A very different example comes from a study I just completed observing community college occupational programs as varied as fashion and diesel technology. As students developed competence, they also became more committed to doing a job well, were better able to monitor and correct their performance, and im-proved their ability to communicate what they were doing and help others do it. You could be by inclina-tion the most determined or communicative person in the world, but if you don't know what you're doing with a garment or an engine, your tendencies won't be realized in a meaningful way in the classroom or the workshop.

Also, we have to consider the consequences of this cognitive/noncognitive binary in light of the history of American educational practice. We have a power-ful tendency toward either/or policies—think of old math/new math or phonics/whole language. Given this tendency, we can predict a pendulum swing away from the academic and toward character education. And over the past fifty years attempts at character edu-cation as a distinct pursuit have not been particularly successful—in some cases, student behavior is not affected, or changes in beliefs and behaviors don't last.

Finally, the focus of the current character education movement is on low-income children, and the cold, hard fact is that many poor kids are already getting terrible educations in the cognitive domain. There's a stirring moment in Paul Tough's book where a remarkable chess teacher decides she's going to try to prepare one of her star pupils for an admissions test for New York's selective high schools. What she found was that this stunningly bright boy had learned pitifully little academic knowledge during his eight years in school. It would be tragic to downplay a strong academic education for children like him.

This example brings to the fore my second concern about the current championing of character education. When the emphasis on character is focused on the individual attributes of poor children as the reason for their subpar academic performance, it can remove broader policies to address poverty and educational inequality from public discussion.

One of the powerful strands in the current discussion of character education is that it might succeed where academic interventions have failed in reducing the achievement gap. Perhaps psychological and educational interventions that focus on developing perseverance, self-control, and the like will help poor children succeed in school. Such qualities are indisputably key to a successful life, and they've been part of our folk wisdom about success well before Dale Carnegie made millions by promoting the power of positive thinking. But they've gained luster via economic modeling, psychological studies, and the technological advances of neuroscience. Because brain imaging allows us to see the frontal lobes light up when someone weighs a decision, these claims about character seem cutting edge. It is this aura of the new that contributes to a belief that we might have found a potent treatment for the achievement gap.

A diverse group of players is involved in this rediscovery and championing of character. Nobel Laureate in economics James Heckman advocates early childhood intervention programs for poor kids. Some charter schools, KIPP among them, infuse character education throughout the school day. And a whole range of smaller extracurricular and after-school programs—from Chicago's OneGoal to a chess club in a public school in Brooklyn—focus their efforts in helping the children of the poor develop a range of mental strategies and shifts in perception aimed toward academic achievement. I have worked with economically and educationally disadvantaged children and adults for forty years and know the importance of efforts such as these. They need to be funded and expanded, for poor kids carry a heavy load and have absurdly limited access to any kind of school-related enrichment, especially as inequality widens.

But we have to be very careful, given the political tenor of our time, not to assume that we have the long-awaited key to helping the poor overcome the assaults of poverty. My worry is that we will embrace these essentially individual and technocratic fixes—mental conditioning for the poor—and abandon broader social policy aimed at poverty itself.

We have a long-standing shameful tendency in America to attribute all sorts of pathologies to the poor. Writing in the mid-nineteenth century, the authors of a report from the Boston School Committee bemoaned the "undisciplined, uninstructed . . . inveterate forwardness and obstinacy" of their working-class and immigrant students. There was much talk in the Boston Report and elsewhere about teaching the poor "self-control," "discipline," "earnestness," and "planning for the future." This language is way too familiar.

Some poor families are devastated by violence, uprooting, and substance abuse, and children are terribly affected. But some families hold together with iron-willed determination and instill values and habits of mind that middle-class families strive for. There's as much variability among the poor as in any group, and we have to keep that fact squarely in our sights, for we easily slip into one-dimensional generalities about them.

Given a political climate that is antagonistic toward the welfare state and has further shredded our already compromised safety net, psychosocial intervention may be the only viable political response to poverty available. But can you imagine the outcry if, let's say, an old toxic dump were discovered near Scarsdale or Beverly Hills, and the National Institutes of Health undertook a program to teach kids strategies to lessen the effects of the toxins but didn't do anything to address the dump itself?

We seem willing to accept remedies for the poor that we are not willing to accept for anyone else. We should use our science to figure out why that is so—and then develop the character and courage to fully address poverty when it is an unpopular cause.

EIGHT

Reflections on Standards, Teaching, and Learning

STANDARDS ARE CRITERIA used to judge competence, and we rely on them every day, all the time: in sports or cooking, in raising children or voting, in forming relationships or teaching school. Another basic truth about standards is that we argue about them. This is surely true in education, where standards have a contentious history.

When I was working in programs for underprepared high school and college students back in the 1980s, a national debate emerged over standards, expressed as a conflict between equity—increasing access to higher education—and excellence, holding firm on merit and achievement. The nation then saw the rise of the standards movement, an attempt to articulate precisely what students should know K–12, grade by grade, about history or mathematics or social studies—and to align instruction to these standards.

And this movement led to another set of debates about district or state control versus local autonomy and teacher independence, among other things. An emphasis on accountability then became part of standards talk, and it all intensified considerably with the advent of high-stakes testing, most notably the federal No Child Left Behind Act. These days, all eyes are on Common Core State Standards, which I'll address at the end of this chapter.

Regardless of what one thinks about the merits of any of these concerns about standards, the discourse and debates around them have narrowed and polarized our understanding of standards, the way we define standards and conceive of them in instruction.

We need additional ways to talk about standards if we are to help students develop what educator Mina Shaughnessy calls their "incipient excellence."

Let's start from the specifics of the classroom. Although I hope that what I say applies to other domains, I will ground my discussion on the teaching of writing at the college level and begin with two classroom stories.

Vince, who received a PhD from a prestigious psychology department, tells his story from the enviable position of one who has succeeded in the academy. Coming from a working-class, Mexican American background, Vince learned his first English from a television set, but with his parents' encouragement, he worked hard at his second language, and by high school, he was taking college-preparatory English classes. They were designed to help students do well on achievement tests and the Scholastic Aptitude Test; the classes consisted primarily of workbook grammar exercises, although students also read some literature and wrote a few book reports. After completing high school, Vince figured he was ready for college, so he was stunned when he sat for his university English placement exam: "We were to answer a question on a reading passage, something on the use of grain—and we were supposed to argue for one position or another. 'What the hell am I supposed to write?' I thought. They wanted an argumentative paper, though I didn't know that then. . . . I knew my grammar, but applying it to that kind of writing was another story."

Vince's poor performance landed him in remedial English. As he recalls, "The teacher seemed very distant and cold. I'd get my papers back graded with a C or lower and with red marks about my style all over them." Vince couldn't figure out what the teacher wanted: "I kept trying, but I kept getting the same grades. I went through this routine for four or five weeks, becoming more withdrawn. Finally I said, 'Forget this,' and stopped going to class."

Vince took the class again two quarters later and got a teacher who gave feedback in a more useful way and was more encouraging. He started going to the campus learning center and asked for help from teaching assistants in other courses in which the instructors had assigned papers. He learned to write good academic prose and in graduate school was frequently complimented for his writing.

Vince's story illuminates several problems with how standards are used and misused in the teaching of English. Often, they are reduced to so-called objective measures, like multiple-choice grammar tests, and although the instruction geared toward such measures can be specific and targeted, it is also limited. Vince's high-school English classes had been labeled "college preparatory," so he believed they would prepare him to write in college, but they had not prepared him for even his first university writing assignment, the English placement exam. This discontinuity in requirements and the standards used to assess performance—in this case the shift from grammatical analysis to the development of an effective argument—is common.

In his first college class, Vince faced another problem associated with standards: they often are applied to students' work in ways that shut down rather than foster learning. In Vince's case, the teacher seemed to value a literary style and rejected as inadequate Vince's more straightforward prose. Such teachers match student work against an internalized model of excellence and find the work lacking, rather than using their knowledge of genre, rhetorical strategy, and style to assess the ways a paper could be improved, given what the writer seems to be trying to do. This kind of teacher functions more like a gatekeeper than an educator. Standards used this way become a barrier to development.

The second, briefer, story comes from a remedial English class at an inner-city community college in Los Angeles. About thirty students are enrolled, most of them from working-class backgrounds and a variety of ethnic origins, ranging from Armenian to Salvadoran. The students have been writing educational autobiographies. And one of the interesting issues they raise involves standards. Some express anger at past teachers who didn't hold high expectations for them, who didn't explain the criteria for competence and hold students to them, who didn't help their students master the conventions of written English that they're struggling with now. Some of these teachers sound as though they were burned out, but others seemed reluctant to impose their standards for philosophical or political reasons or because they thought a less rigorous pedagogy was better suited to these students. One teacher, for example, is described as "hang loose," a man who created a pleasant classroom atmosphere but played down the evaluation of students' work.

This episode highlights the important role that standards and high expectations play in good teaching. It also clarifies why so many educators and parents from poor or nondominant communities—though mindful of the injustices that can occur in the name of standards—are calling for classrooms in which standards are clearly articulated and maintained. Standards that are employed fairly facilitate learning and show students that their teachers believe in their ability to meet academic expectations.

People leery about calls for standards need to remember their benefits and reclaim them for democratic ends, despite the fact that standards and assessments can be used to limit access and stratify students into educational tracks, or can lead to an overly prescriptive and narrow curriculum. At the same time, the champions of standards need to take a closer look at how standards and our means of measuring student mastery of them can limit, rather than advance, the intellectual development they desire.

To develop our fuller discussion about standards, we must hold Vince's story about the misapplication of standards and the community college students' tale of low expectations simultaneously in mind, in productive tension. As we do so, some questions emerge.

The current drive to enact and enforce standards by statistical measures dominates schooling. But what effects do such measures have on instruction? As people on many sides of current educational debates are saying, standardized measures can limit the development of competence by driving curricula toward the narrow demands of test preparation instead of allowing teachers to immerse students in complex problem solving and rich use of language.

How good are we at explaining our standards to students? Too much teaching is like the instruction Vince encountered in his first remedial course: teachers match a response or product against an inadequately explained criterion of excellence. To avoid such stifling imposition of standards and to encourage student expression, some teachers refrain from applying their criteria of effective performance. But this can be problematic as well, for many students report that they feel cheated, and sometimes baffled, by such instruction.

How can we reconceive standards so that they function not just as final measures of competence but also as guides to improving performance? Many discussions of standards stay at the level of test scores or models of excellence. Instead of these static measures of attainment, our focus should shift to the dynamics of development. Such a shift would have led Vince's first teacher to make explicit the distinctions he saw between his criteria and his student's performance. He also would have tried to understand the possibilities of Vince's own style and helped Vince enhance it with some stylistic options drawn from the teacher's more elaborate repertoire.

What about the transitions students face as they move from one level of the educational system to another? Are the standards we use coherent—that is, is there some level of agreement between secondary and postsecondary institutions about what constitutes competence in a given discipline? What opportunities exist—for example, through college-school alliances—that would help us articulate areas of agreement and disagreement so that students like

Vince don't find themselves baffled by very different kinds of curricula and sets of expectations?

How reflective are we about the attitudes and assumptions that underlie our standards? How open are we to considering the provisional nature of these standards and modifying them? In writing instruction, for example, teachers sometimes judge students' work according to idealized models of composing that distort actual practice, or some teachers champion the "great tradition of English prose" without considering the many ways that tradition is modified as audiences and purposes shift. What mechanisms are there within teacher education and professional development to encourage such reflection?

———————

Curriculum specialists come to consensus about what students should know about a particular subject—photosynthesis, for example, or the Civil War. In the cases we just saw involving freshman composition, an exemplary program would engage in discussion about the kind of writing students need to master, the important conventions of that writing, criteria for competence, and so on.

Underlying these issues is a more basic set of

questions: what is the role of a particular subject area in cognitive development? Why do we study it? How does it fit into our philosophy of education? On average, such questions come up less often in the process of forming standards. In some cases, the answers to them are assumed—of course students need to know the facts of photosynthesis. Also, in this age of high-stakes testing, the pressure to cut to the chase is intense—the push is to do the technical work of setting standards. But the basic questions are equally important, for they get to the heart of why we educate in the first place.

During the time I was working on this essay, an article appeared in the *Atlantic Monthly* that raised for me these basic questions about subject matter and instruction. The article deals with college students, but I think it contains lessons about standards and teaching that run across the educational pipeline. The piece is written by Professor X, who teaches freshman composition and introduction to literature at a community college and a small private college. His courses are required, and his students are a diverse, nontraditional group, people who enroll to advance at work: criminal justice, health care, civil service.

The purpose of his article is to challenge the notion that everyone should go to college, and the professor

supports his claim with a narrative of student in-
competence. His students can't write about Joyce's
"Araby" or Faulkner's "Barn Burning." They can't
write a research paper presenting two sides of a historical controversy (why Truman removed MacArthur, for
example). They haven't read a book in common. This
is the stuff of the classic debate on standards—access
and equity versus excellence—and the professor uses
a familiar story line to present it: the beleaguered
teacher fighting the good fight against ignorance.

The professor doesn't come across as a bad guy, and
he frets over the grades he doles out. But what struck
me—and a lot of other readers—is that he seems
clueless about alternative ways to both enact his standards and engage his students in the humanities, to
help them become more effective critical readers and
writers. Nor does he seem to grant them much experience or intelligence that could be brought to bear on
core topics in the humanities. He appears to be a bit
like the instructor that Vince encountered in his first
English composition class.

Standards, particularly in the newer sense of curricular goals aligned to instruction, are a systematic
means of specifying what students should learn. But
there are other ways to be systematic as well. I want
to think about the interaction of subject matter,

teaching, and learning in a way that honors the standards impulse, but comes at it in a different way, that
methodically considers the broader questions of the
purpose of teaching a particular subject (in this case,
literature), why and how we teach it, its connection
to intellectual development and human experience,
our beliefs about intelligence and about teaching, and
what our goals might be, our expectations. Articles like
the one in the *Atlantic Monthly* often use examples from
literature and the humanities, so I'll focus on James
Joyce's "Araby," one of the stories the professor tells
us that his students didn't much like or understand.

"Araby," the third story in Joyce's *Dubliners*, has become part of the Western literary canon, a familiar
entry in countless anthologies. It was on the introduction to humanities syllabus I was given to teach thirty
years ago.

"Araby" is set in Joyce's dreary early-twentieth-
century Dublin and is narrated in the first person by
an adolescent boy who is thoroughly infatuated with
the older sister of one of his pals. The boy's language
is rich, fervid, and his description of his friend's sister is flat-out rapturous. Though he watches her from
afar and only directly encounters her once in the story,
"[his] body was like a harp and her words and gestures

were like fingers running upon the wires." You get the idea.

The defining moment in the story begins to develop when the girl, in that single encounter, expresses regret that she can't go to Araby, the bazaar in town, and our narrator, emboldened, says he will go and bring her something. After an agony of waiting for his drunken uncle to come home with a few shillings, the boy rushes to Araby, arriving at closing time. It is as dreary a place as the city surrounding it. He finds an open booth, eyes vases and tea sets, feels the few coins in his pocket, and realizes suddenly, painfully, the foolhardiness of his desire and quest. "I saw myself as a creature driven and derided by vanity," the story ends, "and my eyes burned with anguish and anger."

There are a lot of things to consider in selecting any piece of literature for a syllabus. Certainly, one's own pleasure with the text matters—it enlivens the teaching—but there needs to be further justification, since teaching literature means reading a story or poem with others to some pedagogical end, a social intellectual activity. Here are some of the things I would think about as I considered assigning "Araby."

I'd ask myself what it is I want to achieve through teaching the story, and these goals would be the stuff of instructional standards. What about literature and the appreciation of it do I want students to learn? What about the structure of the short story? Or Joyce and his Dublin? Or symbolism and imagery? Or conceptions of romance and gender? And I'd ask these questions if I were teaching "Araby" to a group of high schoolers or to a graduate seminar in English—though, of course, the specifics of what I did in each classroom would be different.

I'd intersect such questions with what I know about the students before me, high schoolers to advanced graduate students. Some of what I know comes from their location in the system. Were there prerequisite courses? What have they already been reading for me? And some of what I know is provided by their performance, by discussion in class, by tests or papers, by comments made in conference. Finally, some of what I know emerges via relation, through what I learn about them as people with histories, interests and curiosities, hopes for the future.

Honoring the histories of the people in the class brings into focus another set of, not unrelated, questions, questions about the politics and sociology of what gets selected into literary canons, of what authors get read. These questions belong in a discussion about standards. So I'd be asking myself: does my syllabus reflect in some way, to some degree, the cultural histories of the students before me, particularly if those histories have typically been absent from the curriculum? There can be great pedagogical power here, and anyone who has taught literature has seen it: students lighting up when they read stories with familiar languages, geographies, family scenes, or cultural practices that they haven't read before in a classroom. Given this perspective, and depending on who was in my class, I might take a pass on "Araby." I know that when I first read the story as a college freshman, it seemed as flat and distant as could be. There are many other stories that would enable me to reach my goals about literary technique.

But culture is a complex business, as is teaching. While being responsive to students' cultural histories and practices, we have to be mindful of how easily "culture" can be narrowed and reduced as we try to define it. Education scholar Manuel Espinoza, a former student of mine, says it well: there is "no monolithic us," no blanket African American, or working-class, or Puerto Rican culture, and thus no ready matchup to writers from these backgrounds. Black kids won't automatically respond to Alice Walker. How a story of hers is taught becomes a key variable.

So maybe "Araby" shouldn't be ruled out . . .

Which leads me to a third frame of reference I'd use when considering "Araby." And that is my own experience with the story: as an underprepared college freshman from a working-class background, as someone who later taught "Araby," and as a middle-aged man reading it once again in preparation to write this essay.

As I noted a moment ago, I didn't like "Araby" the first time I read it. Though I had a terrific senior high school English teacher—and some wonderful teachers later in college—my college freshman English instructor was awful. As I subsequently learned more about literary technique in general, and Joyce in particular, and especially as I eventually had to teach "Araby" myself, I came to appreciate it. And reading the story now and thinking back to my own adolescence, it touches me deeply.

I take a few lessons from this brief survey of my own time with "Araby." If I did elect to teach the story, I would consider in hindsight what didn't happen with me upon first encounter—which provides another way to think about how to open the story up to others and my goals for doing so.

I missed completely in my freshman year the overlay of the story with my own experience. Like the narrator, I too lived in a sad and taxing place and sought release in my imagination. And, like him, I had a desperate and unrequited crush—in my case on a waitress in the Mexican restaurant down the street. My heart picked up speed just walking past the front window, hoping that she was at the counter. The important point here is that we sometimes don't see connection or relevance automatically, readily. This is the place where artful teaching comes in.

Teaching also comes in, of course, in understanding literary technique, the way "Araby" works as a story: the structure of the thing, the boy's hyperbolic language, the small touches that mean so much. I remember not getting the ending at all: how did we go so quickly from looking at vases and jingling a few coins in the pocket to the crashing "my eyes burned with anguish and anger"? But a little guided reflection on that ending would have revealed a powerful truth, surely known to me as a teenager, and, for that fact, to all the students in the anonymous professor's class: that our hopes are sometimes dashed through the smallest thing—an overheard remark, a glance away, an opportunity missed by a minute or two. Now, we are at the heart of what literature can provide: an imaginative entry to human experience.

John Dewey makes this observation about subject matter: "[T]he various studies represent working resources, available capital . . . [yet] the teacher should be occupied not with subject matter in itself but in its interaction with the pupils' present needs and capabilities." Dewey reminds us of the intimate and powerful relationship between a subject (literature, or biology, or geography) and human development—with teaching as the mediating force. Standards and expectations are a crucial part of the dynamic, though that dynamic can become distorted if we hold to a rigid conceptualization of standards or get consumed in the technical development of them. It is finally our philosophy of education, our fundamental justification for schooling, that gives standards—any definition of standards—their meaning.

With these thoughts on standards as backdrop, let me consider the newest incarnation of standards, Common Core State Standards. Emerging out of the standards and accountability movement of the past few decades, Common Core Standards begin to take shape in 2009 when the National Governors Association joined by the Council of Chief State School Officers hired a young consultant with a strong humanities background, David Coleman, to spearhead the development of K–12 curriculum standards in language arts and mathematics that would lead to a more demanding course of study, to "deep learning" that would make students "college and career ready." In essence, these standards would require students to think about and use what they're learning rather than only demonstrating that they've learned a fact or process. So, for example, students should be able to not only read a fiction or nonfiction text but also discuss and write about it using passages from the text to support their claims.

The standards were written and presented such that they could be adopted by the states, resulting in more national regularity in curriculum and assessment. If successful, these standards would lead to better-prepared students, which would reduce the need for college-level remediation. The assessments connected to the standards could provide an objective measure of college readiness, which could be used for college admissions and course placement. Thus Common Core could be a mechanism to bring into alignment the many moving parts of our kindergarten-through-college educational system. A grand vision.

Standards come and go. Some district offices have multiple sets of them in thick binders on back-wall shelves. But Common Core had powerful backers in those governors and increasingly garnered major philanthropic support. President Obama's Department of Education turbocharged adoption of Common Core by making adoption of "college and career ready" standards (such as Common Core) a precondition for Race to the Top applications, and also for waivers from NCLB requirements. As of mid-2013, forty-five states and the District of Columbia have adopted Common Core Standards, and their implementation is to begin in the 2014–15 school year. This is a remarkable achievement, given our country's historical resistance to anything resembling a national curriculum—a resistance that could reemerge as new governors take over statehouses.

Opinions about Common Core vary widely. One exceptional principal I know who has been deeply involved with Common Core says that "this is what education is supposed to be. After waiting my whole career, I have a chance to see it." Another friend, also terrifically talented and in education for the long haul, sees the potential of the standards but fears that the whole enterprise is quickly becoming "the Educational-Industrial Complex." I think that some of the diversity of opinion—though by no means all—comes from what part of the Common Core movement you examine. Let us revisit some of the people we met earlier to help us explore these different dimensions of Common Core. We'll start with Vince.

Vince, you'll remember, was the fellow whose high school English classes were designed to prepare him for college, but, in fact, didn't prepare him for his freshman composition placement exam, which required him to write an argument using a nonfiction text. It is exactly this disconnect between segments of the educational system that Common Core hopes to address. Also, under Common Core, Vince would have had more experience writing from specific texts, both fiction and nonfiction. Whether you like or loathe the kind of writing exam Vince encountered, at least it would not have been unfamiliar to him. Then there were those students we met in the community college classroom, the ones who regretted not having a more rigorous high school English curriculum, the kind Common Core could yield—perhaps leading to fewer of them being held for remedial English.

What about Professor X and his classes of people he doubts should be in college? A number of the adults in Professor X's classrooms are long out of high school, but, for the sake of argument, let's imagine them back in junior or senior year with similar levels of familiarity with the humanities and similar motivations for being in school. This situation will be widespread as Common Core is fully implemented. Students who will experience Common Core from the primary grades on will be well prepared for a curriculum like Professor X's, but a number of those who move into Common Core in middle and high school will need additional support to meet the standards' level of expectation. And those who teach these students might well need high-quality professional development not only to get in the Common Core groove but also to adapt and adjust the curriculum and the way it's taught for the students struggling with it— what Professor X should have done. Fueled by Race to the Top grants, a number of agencies and consortia are producing terrific materials for Common Core, and those will help teachers new to the standards a great deal. But it would be naïve to think that materials taken off the Web—no matter how good—will alone enable teachers to help less-than-prepared students meet the challenges of Common Core.

Then there's "Araby." Though Common Core does not offer grade-by-grade recommendations for readings—that's the individual state's role—it did cause an early flap by recommending a good proportion of nonfiction, "informational" texts in the curriculum, particularly across the curriculum, since the aim is to have science, social science, and mathematics teachers attend to the literacy demands within their subject areas. Still, there was an outcry that reached the broader media when the preeminence of literature in the English curriculum was threatened. Underlying these concerns lies the humanist's deep faith in the moral and imaginative power of literature. Would "Araby" be replaced by a technical report from OSHA?

In defense of Common Core's advocacy of nonfiction texts, both across the curriculum and within the English classroom, I can say that when I was working in those tutorial and preparatory programs, my co-workers and I routinely encountered students who could speak or write moderately well about a play or short story, but were at a loss with readings in history or sociology. So we developed our own curriculum both to integrate reading and writing into those disciplines and to teach students how to critically read and write about nonfiction texts.

There is a broader question underlying Common Core, a question raised throughout this book: what kind of education benefits a democracy brimming with a diversity of interests, motivations, abilities? Common Core Standards reflect a traditional liberal studies approach to the school curriculum: a close attention to written texts, an emphasis on the reasoning behind a claim or an answer in mathematics, an attention to precision in writing and speaking, and so on. The advocates of Common Core see it as an egalitarian curriculum, a kind of college prep curriculum for all. I favor this position, having worked my whole professional life toward a similar end. But there is another perspective to consider here, and it is the other element in an American debate that is more than a century old. While it may seem democratic to give a similar curriculum to everyone, it is democratic as well to respond to the varied needs and interests of the students who fill our classrooms, some of whom simply are not the least bit taken by the liberal arts, no matter how well taught. So an academic curriculum meant to increase retention and achievement in school could have the opposite effect. As Anthony Carnevale, the director of Georgetown's Center on Education and the Workforce, quipped about efforts like Common Core, maybe what we need is not only "Math for Harvard" but also "Math for Heating, Ventilation, and Air-Conditioning." As I discussed in chapter 5, "Intelligence in the Workplace and the Schoolhouse," this second perspective can lead to curricular tracking, but it can also lead us to think more carefully, as John Dewey did, about the mathematical (or literate or scientific) possibilities in occupations.

Debates about the content of curriculum standards are to be expected, and, in fact, can be generative, leading to a richer course of study and creative teaching. But the other piece of the enterprise, the machine at the core of implementation, is assessment, and many who differ in their opinion of the standards agree that the thing that will make or break Common Core is the quality of assessment. Earlier, I quoted a principal who is an avid supporter of Common Core; her big concern involves assessment, for testing done too soon or with the wrong instruments "could kill the movement." Her concerns about testing bring her closer to the other veteran educator who fears the Educational-Industrial Complex.

There are good reasons to worry, given recent history. Many of the early supporters of Common Core saw it as an antidote to the reductive tendencies of NCLB, but some are now worried that those tendencies could be repeated. How soon will policy makers expect positive outcomes? We are a country that expects quick results, and in the contentious, high-pressure world of school reform, that expectation will not be easy to temper. Furthermore, will the demands of policy makers for precise metrics (needed for statistical evaluation of teacher effectiveness, for example) force a reductive assessment of bits and pieces of the curriculum rather than the "core knowledge and skills" advocated by the architects of Common Core?

There is a lot of faith being put into the development of assessments for Common Core, but the fact is that we don't have the testing technology that can validly measure many of the kinds of rich, complex thinking that is at the heart of Common Core. It is very much an open question as to whether or not we can develop such tests—at least in the ways that would mesh with high-stakes, broad-scale accountability. One illustration of my concern is the brief writing sample that is part of the current assessment plan. The sample will be scored by a computer, based on certain semantic and syntactic features in the writing. It's doubtful that this approach gets to "deep learning" rather than simply providing a count of the features a computer can detect. It is these assessments that will also determine if someone is "college ready," so you can see why some in higher education are raising red flags. These objections could be dismissed as turf protection and one more example of the rigidity of our educational institutions. But when those who teach writing object that you can't determine readiness for the writing demands of college through counts of isolable features of text, they have a legitimate point.

Then there is the issue of funding. The money assisting Common Core from philanthropies and Race to the Top will not last, so where will the resources come from to maintain Common Core? The hope is that the market will take over as publishing and testing companies assume the expense and risk of full-scale implementation. But markets easily put profits over educational interests, and that basic truth has generated some of the deepest suspicions about Common Core. There is big money to be made if you have most states adopting one accountability system rather than state-by-state systems. We live in a capitalist economy, so the publishing and testing industries are simply a part of mass education, and have been for some time. But critics point to the scale of the Common Core enterprise; the monopoly that a few megacorporations will have on curricular materials and assessment; the fact that some of the philanthropies that contributed to Common Core are connected to high-tech companies that could also profit; and the recent appointment of the chief architect of Common Core, Mr. Coleman, to the head of the College Board with plans of revising the SAT to reflect the standards he created. If Occupy Wall Street activists set out to write a screenplay about all this, they couldn't be handed better material.

So the big question as we move forward with Common Core is whether the political demands and the technical limitations of assessment, combined with the profit motive, will end up driving the curriculum, thereby repeating the troubling pattern we saw develop under other high-stakes accountability programs, particularly NCLB. A "triumph of system over substance," as my wary friend puts it.

Curriculum standards provide guidance on what students need to know and be able to do, but also, at their best, offer a vision of education. The liberal studies orientation of Common Core is certainly not new, but because of the considerable consensus that developed around it, Common Core promised a significant change in an NCLB-dominated landscape. It is the vision of Common Core that excites those teachers who have been working to bring it to a full range of students, not only those who are the most poised to receive it.

Ideally, the cluster of questions I posed when considering "Araby"—from how to encourage a close reading of a difficult text to the complex interaction between student background and literary selection—would be the kinds of questions generated among teachers by Common Core. The fatal flaw in the development of our thinking about standards is the belief that they need to be both put into practice and measured through high-stakes standardized tests, that the tests will ensure proper implementation—"incentivize" it. But these kinds of tests run the risk of undermining the very spirit of Common Core: a clash of a technocratic and a humanistic conception of learning.

The ultimate test of Common Core—and an object lesson for standards-based accountability in general—will be which conception of learning carries the day.

NINE

MOOCs and Other Wonders:
Education and High-Tech Utopia

DEEP WITHIN OUR CULTURAL HISTORY is a faith in the power of technology to cure social problems. Many of our utopian visions—from nineteenth-century socialist tracts and novels to Silicon Valley's libertarian futurism—are based on technology. That faith is vibrant today, at times idealistic, at times entrepreneurial, often a blend of the two. Neuroscience will lead to the cure of mental illness and reveal the mystery of consciousness itself. Social media will bring us together across regional and national divides, and the cell phone or tablet computer will provide the platform to lift people in developing countries out of poverty. And, closer to the concerns of this book, online instruction will reduce the cost and improve the quality of education, and high-stakes standardized tests will scientifically measure student learning and teacher effectiveness.

Modern technology, of course, is stunning, and can and should be brought to bear on our social problems, education included. Those who believe deeply in technology's virtues have reasons for their grand vision. They are well educated and highly skilled in technology's devices and systems, and the arguments they offer are articulate and assured. Their education at prestigious schools provides them with potent social networks that contribute to their access to power and philanthropic and venture capital resources. They are positioned to make things happen.

The limitations—and, in some cases I think, dangers—of this faith in technology are contained within its strengths.

The faith in technology can lead to overreach, to a belief that complex human problems can be framed as engineering problems, their social and political messiness factored away. Hand-in-glove is an epistemological insularity, a lack of knowledge about social and cultural conditions—or worse, a willful discounting of those conditions as irrelevant. It is telling how rarely one hears any references to history or culture in the technologists' discourse. I think the social position of many of the technologists is a factor here: they tend to come from, at the least, middle-class or professional families, and their schooling has sheltered them from intimate knowledge of many of the people they seek to help. Reform movements have often drawn on such elites, and they can bring much-needed resources and power to the reform, but their backgrounds can also blind them to conditions on the ground, to the lives they hope to affect.

I want to consider this faith in technology as it relates to education, using as my central example MOOCs, or Massive Open Online Courses, which are ever present in higher education news as I write. Even if the appeal of the MOOC fades, the issues it raises will be with us for quite a while.

A MOOC is essentially a prerecorded course, heavy on lecture, so, in that regard, it is not at all new. But it is placed online, making it available to anyone with an Internet connection. The first MOOCs originated in Canada in 2008, then spread to the United States, making a splash as several Ivy League faculty began putting their courses online. "Ivy League for the masses," announced *Time* magazine. As MOOCs have developed over the last few years, lectures have been broken up into modular units—easier to process online—and additional instructional materials have been added along with limited means for participants to interact with faculty and students via an electronic forum. There are also attempts, not without considerable complication, to address the issues of testing, grading, and course credit.

Imagine a guy on a remote ranch in Montana or a young woman in Manila learning electrical engineering from MIT's finest. One catches the idealistic thrill of this idea in Daphne Kohler's TED Talk on MOOCs—Kohler is a distinguished computer scientist at Stanford and a driving force in the MOOC enterprise—as she offers a vision of high-quality education spread across the globe via the Internet, solving the problem of access and availability. Over the last year or so, increasing numbers of colleges and universities have been signing up for MOOCs or even developing their own, and the courses are expanding from the originally top-heavy sciences and engineering to include the social sciences and humanities, and even some remedial courses.

I have been around higher education for a long time, and I can't recall an innovation taking off the way the MOOC has. There are several reasons. The humanitarianism of massive reach and open access across the planet has captured the fancy of big-time public voices, including those on the *New York Times* opinion page. Furthermore, as I mentioned earlier, technological idealism readily morphs with entrepreneurship, and many of the MOOC luminaries have formed both for-profit and nonprofit companies that engage in the hard sell. There is a lot of hype generated around MOOCs: they are part of a "tsunami" or an "avalanche" about to hit higher education—or they are higher education's "Napster moment." A third, and huge, factor is that college administrators and state legislators see MOOCs as a way to reduce the soaring costs of higher education as well as to provide access to high-demand classes.

Amid the enthusiasm, there are many concerns about MOOCs, some of which are a function of their rapid spread, from technical and infrastructural problems (predictable when enrollment is in the tens of thousands), to issues of intellectual property, to grading and credit (if I'm at the University of Tennessee and complete a Harvard course in my computer science major, does that course transfer to my new institution?), to questions of the role and status of faculty at receiving institutions (what role do the computer science faculty and graduate students at Tennessee play if the university subscribes to multiple courses, and will their ranks diminish over time?). These are complex issues that may or may not get worked out if MOOCs continue to spread and develop.

But here, I'm particularly concerned with the quality of education possible with MOOCs. As MOOCs grow, it's fair to assume there will be a predictable range of faculty talent, but let's give the benefit of the doubt here and grant that MOOC developers will seek skillful teachers. Then the question becomes how well the developers use the considerable capability of instructional technology within the constraints of a *massive* and *open* course that, after all, is still a series of modularized lectures. (Some of the stronger critiques of MOOCs come from experts in educational technology who see the MOOC as a fairly primitive form of online instruction.) This technical question rests on two more basic questions that I don't hear raised much by advocates: what assumptions about learning and what philosophy of education inform the technology?

Perhaps the most frequent criticism of MOOCs comes from college faculty themselves, and, for shorthand, I'll call it the humanistic argument: education involves more than watching a lecture on the computer, even if enhanced with options for interaction. What about the spontaneous give-and-take between teacher and student or student and student? What about the teacher's in-the-moment assessment of classroom dynamics? This concern, of course, reflects a broader tension of our time between electronic connection versus human touch. The MOOC advocates have several answers to the humanistic argument. The first is that with the right technology, certain kinds of interaction between teachers, teachers' assistants, and students are achievable and exist in some MOOCs now. But this interaction occurs within a number of constraints. To my knowledge, no current MOOC encourages a direct exchange between student and professor.

The second counterargument is more convincing, sadly so. The appealing pedagogical portrait conjured in the humanistic complaint is rare when one looks across the full range of classrooms in American higher education. Many students sit through classes that are poorly taught and/or sit in large rooms passively receiving lecture after lecture—if they come to class at all. A well-constructed MOOC would clearly be an improvement. And, a genuine advantage, they could be taken by the increasing numbers of students in American higher education who are older, work, or have families. These students have long provided a powerful rationale for online learning in general, and for-profit virtual colleges (such as the University of Phoenix) have targeted them. It is an egalitarian move, then, for less expensive public colleges to open their doors electronically via MOOCs and other online courses, as some have been doing.

The problem, though, is that at this point in mid-2013, the completion rate for MOOCs is a dreary 10 percent, and what data we have suggest that many of the people who do complete the courses are people who already hold degrees. Rather than fulfilling the promise of MOOCs providing an entryway to an elite education for the masses, so far they serve as an enrichment for the educated—not a bad thing by any means, but different from the liberating vision of Professor Kohler's TED Talk. Some strong advocates of MOOCs are beginning to dial down expectations a notch.

MOOCs are in their early stages, so the situation is fluid, but if the above data are any indication of demographics and persistence, the prospect of the widespread use of MOOCs in the potentially cost-saving areas of introductory and remedial courses is troubling. To be sure, there is an important role electronic technology can play—is already playing—in such classes, from graphic enhancements to interactive tutorials to platforms enabling and enhancing teacher-student and student-student interaction. But the digital divide is still very much with us, so even tech-savvy students who are poor or who live in remote areas will have trouble both with infrastructure and equipment. I saw such problems continually in inner-city community colleges. And I also witnessed a related difficulty: older students who were not comfortable with the computer avoided or dropped classes that contained any online component. The whole world is not wired.

Earlier I mentioned the central importance of a theory of learning and philosophy of education when considering the creation and distribution of MOOCs. There is currently a major rethinking of remedial education underway, as well as important discussions about undergraduate education, the role of the humanities, scientific literacy, and more. These discussions are taking place apace with the development of MOOCs, and occasionally serve as material in critical appraisals of MOOCs, but I don't see these core educational concerns embedded within the rapid development of MOOCs themselves.

What we do have is a fevered and, at least for now, ever-present debate on the business, technology, and infrastructure of the enterprise. But questions about the purpose of education and the way people learn should be integral to the technical and infrastructural deliberations, and the fact that they're not is partly a reflection of the technological orientation that fuels the MOOC juggernaut. It is telling that the one

discussion of learning that we do hear is a terribly reductive one—and it emerges from the promise of "big
data" and "data analytics," another element of our era's
technological fixation. Because so many students will
be responding to instructional materials and taking
tests, the reasoning goes, we will have truckloads of
data on, for example, how many people choose what
test answer; we can then find correlations among these
choices to see if one teaching method rather than another yields better scores. This approach—and it is
offered with great enthusiasm—is riddled with problems. If the past is prologue, the tests will be multiple
choice (for physics or for poetry), so we have only a
narrow kind of learning and testing to begin with.
Furthermore, seeking correlations among multiple-
choice answers will give us at best a slew of low-to-
modest relationships among test items that will tell
us nothing about how students are thinking, or what
about a particular thing a professor does leads to the
correlation. And in line both with the faith in big data
and the insularity of technological utopianism, there
is not even an acknowledgment—and possibly no
awareness—of the century's worth of research done
by psychologists, anthropologists, and educators on
learning. This absence could be a function of disci-
plinary insularity, but I also think something else is

in play, something we see in other domains of contemporary education reform: a dismissal of anything smacking of traditional education, schools of education, or educational research.

One reason we don't hear much extended, historically informed discussion of learning and the purpose of a college education is that such issues are not central to the technological orientation I've been discussing. Another is because the main force driving the rush to MOOCs by administrators and legislators is the prospect of saving money. MOOCs in, let's say, introductory calculus, psychology, and geology could replace individual offerings on multiple campuses, with resulting reductions in faculty—or at least an economical transformation of their roles. In a measured book, *Higher Education in the Digital Age*, a former president of Princeton, William Bowen, rightly warns of the public backlash that will occur if the rapidly rising cost of higher education is not reined in. He sees digital technologies, MOOCs among them, as one promising way to contain costs—though he urges caution and research on implementation.

As Bowen admits, the soaring cost of a college education has multiple causes, and a big one is the significant disinvestment of states in public higher education—more than a 20 percent decrease since the 1980s. Whether MOOCs could make a worthwhile difference against such a deficit is an open question. There is another cluster of economic and social issues that MOOCs, if they do take off, could affect, and I'd like to bring this chapter to a close by considering those issues: an interweaving of technology, economics, and prestige and status.

As an example, let's consider a currently popular MOOC, Harvard political philosopher Michael Sandel's introductory-level course "Justice." Sandel is a distinguished scholar and a fine lecturer: articulate with good presence, able to explain political philosophy cogently. But, and I mean no disrespect in saying this, what he does is good, strong traditional lecturing; it is a wonderful skill built on a life of study. But others also do it well, and they aren't all in the Ivy League; in fact, my high-school senior English teacher and my college philosophy instructor were equally skilled. The MOOC, as conceived now, plays into the pronounced status distinctions among institutions in American higher education—something that itself should be the focus of discussion as we try to continually move the American system toward the egalitarian vision that allegedly defines it. Imagine, as a thought experiment, that a smart and articulate physicist or philosopher from a state college in the Midwest had done one of the first American MOOCs. You can bet that the *New York Times* crowd would not have written about it and high-tech philanthropies and venture capitalists would not have showered it with money.

Equally troubling is that the MOOC also reinforces the phenomenon of the celebrity academic, the "star" and "superstar" (even, God help us, "rock star"), words you'll hear increasingly in academic circles. The fact that the academy has so readily embraced the vocabulary and social dynamics of celebrity culture should be a source of shame and ridicule; instead, such celebrity is advanced by the MOOC enterprise.

When you consider the institutional sources of MOOCs and the direction of their distribution, a troubling pattern emerges: the MOOCs originate primarily in elite universities and flow down the status ladder to other less prestigious schools. Seen in an idealistic light, this is a delivery of an "Ivy League education to the masses." But if done in a way that preserves faculty at elite institutions—even enhances those institutions—while possibly contributing to the reduction of faculty at receiving institutions, and ipso facto, a worsening of student-to-faculty ratio—well, then, you've got the dynamics of inequality at work once again: a supposed egalitarian move increasing the inequality in the kinds of education less privileged students receive. An idealistic intent, as history has repeatedly demonstrated, plays out in real-world economic and sociopolitical contexts, and those contexts can distort, even reverse, an idealistic purpose.

In the college of the future—and the future is already here—we will most likely see some variation of a MOOC along with other online modes of instruction. And traditional classrooms will be enhanced by various electronic platforms to aid in everything from presenting course materials, to facilitating discussion, to keeping records. The fundamental question is how all these media and formats will be integrated into a comprehensive and coherent course of study. The problem with MOOCs right now is that they are being heralded as yet another technological wonder to save us from a web of complex social and educational problems: rising costs, shrinking budgets, overcrowding, and restricted access. For all the caveats and disclaimers that everyone on all sides of any educational reform issue keeps offering about there being no miracle cure, no magic bullet, we keep rushing toward them, solemnly intoning that there is no quick fix—and at the next press conference announcing the new game-changer. When will we stop this distracting

and, in fact, expensive worship of the new technological system or device and settle into the less enthralling
but more substantial recognition that MOOCs—or
any other wonder, from digital games to the most recent statistical procedure—will only be as useful as
the thinking about their use, the depth of learning
we want to achieve, the kind of education we want to
foster.

TEN

Re-mediating Remediation

KEVIN HAD A STORY similar to a lot of young men from my old neighborhood. He was a good student in poor schools, schools with dated textbooks, scarce resources for enrichment, high teacher turnover. And like more than a few young men from such neighborhoods, he was seduced by street life, got into trouble, and spent most of his sixteenth year in a juvenile camp.

Upon release, he went back to school, worked hard, graduated, did miserably on the SAT, and went to college through a special admissions program.

I had helped develop the writing component for that program, and I taught in it. Kevin's first piece of college writing—the placement exam—was peppered with grammatical errors, and the writing was disorganized and vague. This is the kind of writing we see in media accounts of remedial students, and it is the kind of writing that academics and politicians cite as an example of how higher education is being compromised. And such writing *is* troubling. If Kevin's writing remained like this, he would probably not make it through college.

The traditional remedial writing course typically begins with simple writing assignments and includes a fair amount of workbook exercises, mostly focused on grammar and usage. The readings used in such a course are also fairly basic, both in style and content. Though they might not be articulated, there are powerful—and limiting—assumptions about language, learning, and cognition that drive such a curriculum: students like Kevin need to go back to linguistic square one, building skill slowly through the elements of grammar. Simple reading and writing assignments won't overly tax Kevin's limited ability and will allow a concentration on correcting linguistic error. Complex, demanding work and big ideas—college work—should be put on hold until Kevin displays mastery of the basics.

No wonder remediation gets such a bad rap.

The program we created for students like Kevin held to a different set of assumptions, which we had come to from reading current research on language and cognition and from our own experience in the classroom. We certainly acknowledged the trouble

Kevin was in and wanted to help him improve his writing on all levels, grammar to organization to style. But
we didn't believe we needed to carve up language into
small workbook bits and slowly, slowly build his skill.
And in Kevin's case, we were right. By the end of the
twenty-week program, Kevin was writing competent
papers explicating poems by Gary Soto and Jim Dan-
iels, comparing the approaches to reading presented
in *The Autobiography of Malcolm X* and Ben Franklin's *Autobiography*, and analyzing the decision making in the
Cuban missile crisis.

My co-workers and I began by surveying a range
of lower-division courses to get a sense of the typical kinds of reading and writing assignments faced by
students like Kevin in that critical first year. We then
found readings from a variety of disciplines that were
similar to those in our survey and created assignments
that helped students develop the skills to write about
them. Then we sequenced the assignments from less
to more difficult and made them cumulative: what a
student learned to do in the first week fed into an
assignment on the fifth. So, for example, early assignments Kevin faced required him to read a passage on
the history of eugenics and write a definition of it,
and to read a passage with diagrams about income
distribution in the United States and summarize it.

This practice in defining and summarizing would later come into play when Kevin had to compare systematically the descriptions of becoming literate in *The Autobiography of Malcom X* and Ben Franklin's *Autobiography*.

To assist students with assignments like these, we organized instruction so that there was lots of discussion of the readings and a good deal of in-class writing where students could try out ideas and get feedback on their work as it developed.

And because many of our students, like Kevin, did display in their writing all the grammatical, stylistic, and organizational problems that give rise to remedial writing courses in the first place, we did spend a good deal of time on error—in class, in conference, on comments on their papers—*but in the context of their academic writing*. This is a huge point and one that is tied to our core assumptions about cognition and language: that writing filled with grammatical error does not preclude engagement with sophisticated intellectual material, and that error can be addressed effectively as one is engaging such material.

Certainly not all students did as well as Kevin, but many did. Those who want to purge college of remedial courses would say that Kevin doesn't belong. He proved them wrong. And those holding to a traditional remedial model would be fearful that the tasks we assigned would be too difficult, would discourage Kevin. He proved them wrong as well.

Since we mounted those programs, some studies have emerged that confirm the approach we took. Successful remedial programs set high standards, are focused on inquiry and problem solving in a substantial curriculum, utilize a pedagogy that is supportive and interactive, draw on a variety of techniques and approaches, and are in line with student goals and provide credit for coursework.

I certainly believe in this approach, have seen it work, have written about it. And I've experienced it. I came out of elementary school with a dreary knowledge of mathematics. Whether the cause was a poor curriculum or uninspired teaching or my own fear of numbers . . . who knows? I didn't pass algebra in high school, had to take it over in the summer, barely passed it then, was mystified by it. And things got worse after that. My SAT quantitative score was awful; my GRE score was even lower, the score of someone barely conscious. Needless to say, I avoided anything even vaguely mathematical through as much of my post–high school education as possible. Then came graduate school in educational psychology and a two-quarter requirement in statistics.

Educational researchers Michael Cole, Peg Griffin, Kris Gutiérrez, and others have a nice way of talking about successful remediation. They refer to re-mediation—that is, changing the environment and the means through which students are taught the material they had not mastered before. This definition certainly characterizes what I tried to do with the remediation programs I developed, and it nicely describes what happened to me with the dreaded statistics.

I realize that my story does not perfectly match the typical remedial tale: I was not taking again a course I had taken earlier in my educational career. But the situation is similar: I had failed, barely passed, or avoided mathematics in the past and was now facing a higher-level course with dismal basic knowledge of mathematics. There's a further point to make here. Remediation occurs in many ways, on many levels, involving most of us at some time or another.

In the summer before I entered graduate school, I signed up for an introductory-level statistics course at UCLA Extension, and I hired a tutor. The course had a clear and meaningful goal for me. And having a tutor provided a huge amount of assistance, some of it in basic math, though in the context of statistics. And—no small thing—she offered a relationship built around mathematics, a human face to a subject that had scared me my whole scholastic life.

I was fortunate in that my graduate courses were taught by an excellent instructor who distributed to us draft chapters of a textbook he was writing, a clear and coherent text. In the text and in lecture, the professor continually provided concrete, real-world examples drawn from education. A few of us in the class formed a study group, providing another social context for learning. And during the first term, I kept in touch with my tutor, providing continuity and further, yes, remediation.

I ended up doing just fine in both statistics courses—to my great pleasure and surprise, I can honestly tell you. So I know the feeling of successful remediation, of re-mediating mathematics in a manner that countered a dozen years of failure and aversion. Of course, I had changed along the way and had powerful motivation to get the stuff this time around. Of course. But the scholastic graveyard is littered with people who wanted desperately to master a topic and didn't. It takes more than desire. A complaint often leveled at remediation by legislators is that they are "paying twice" for instruction in material that should have been learned earlier. Fair enough, but when remediation, re-mediation, is done well, the material in a sense is encountered anew, in a new context, with new curriculum and new pedagogy. For some of us this makes all the difference in the world.

———————

There is a fairly standard media story about remedial education and remedial students. One element of the story portrays remediation as a new phenomenon, an apocalyptic sign of our academic decline. It is true that at some institutions, particularly some community colleges, the numbers have increased, but colleges have been offering some form of remediation to significant numbers of students since before those colleges had yell leaders and fight songs. In the 1890s, 40 percent of colleges and universities had preparatory programs for students who were not yet ready for the standard curriculum.

Another element of the story is one of vast numbers of students mired in remedial math or English courses that they repeatedly fail. There are students like these, for sure. But there are many others with a wide range of profiles in a wide range of institutions. Some are placed in remedial courses and some self-select into them. There are returning students who at one point had mastered the material in question, but need to revisit it. There are immigrant students who are building skill in English. There are students who are seeking new careers or who have served in the military and do need a few basic courses in English and math, but who find their way. And there are students like Kevin who are fresh out of high school with a less-than-privileged education who can catch up with the right intervention.

Do the courses work? Until recently there hasn't been very good evaluation of the effectiveness of remedial courses and programs, but more rigorous research is emerging. The findings are mixed, but do show that for many students who are not severely underprepared (particularly in reading, the core academic skill), remedial courses can make a difference in persistence and success in college. And as for the numbers of courses needed, many students require one or two courses to get up to speed—the remedial domain is not glutted with students hopelessly cycling through multiple courses.

I don't for a moment want to deny the gravity of underpreparation. And I'm not being dismissive about the cost; I spent too many years running programs to be blithe about resources. I also share the dissatisfaction with the kind of curriculum and pedagogy that too often characterizes remedial education. The exciting thing is that currently across the country, inventive two- and four-year college faculty are experimenting with promising new approaches to remediation.

But there is, I think, a broader, important issue here, and that is the place of remediation in a nation that prides itself as being a "second-chance" society. This holds true on both a macrosystems level and on the level of the individual.

There have to be mechanisms in an educational system as vast, complex, and flawed as ours to remedy the *system's* failures. Rather than marginalizing remediation, colleges should invest more intellectual resources into it, making it as serious and effective as it can be. The American college and university no longer defines itself in the classical sense of a place apart from society, an intellectual cloister; the defining word now is "entrepreneurial," and the institution is tied inextricably with government and industry. But there remains, I think, a tendency for colleges and universities to see themselves as detached from the social problems in their environment, and this tendency emerges in discussions of remediation. This orientation is certainly less salient in the community college—which defines itself as "the people's college"—though it is evident in the attitude of some community college faculty in the traditional liberal arts and sciences.

But in an open, vibrant society, the college can't set itself apart, for it is integral to a rich system of human development, reaching down through the schools and well beyond the point of graduation. Colleges and universities honor this connection in a partial way through teacher education, professional programs (e.g., for MBAs), and extension. But the connection is selective, not a fundamental way of conceiving an institution's mission. It *is* a terrible thing that so many students—especially those from poorer backgrounds—come to college unprepared. But colleges can't fold their arms in a huff and try to pull away from the problem. They are embedded in the social and educational surround.

This notion of a second chance, of building safety nets into a flawed system, fits with a democratic and humane definition of the person, one that offers a robust idea of development: the person as changing, coming at something again, fluid, living in a system that acknowledges that people change, retool, grow, need to return to old mistakes, or just to that which is past and forgotten. Remediation may be an unfortunate term for all this, for it carries with it the sense of disease, of a medical intervention. "Something that corrects an evil, a fault, or an error," notes the *American Heritage Dictionary*. But when done well, remediation becomes a key mechanism in a democratic model of human educational development.

ELEVEN

Soldiers in the Classroom

WHAT THE CLASSROOM FULL of veterans wanted most was, as one of them put it, "to help our families understand what we went through." The course was in communication, and it was part of an educational program for veterans of the Vietnam war. The teacher—my colleague in the federally funded program—had asked them what they most wanted to learn, and that was their primary answer: to explain to those closest to them the hell they endured.

Our newest generation of veterans is returning to a warmer welcome than those who served in Vietnam, but the kind of war these veterans fought is similar, and their needs are as great. By one count, over 50,000 have been wounded, some severely, and over 350,000 have been diagnosed with Post-Traumatic Stress Disorder or Traumatic Brain Injury. These and other vets could experience terrible distress as they try to find their way with family and community, the economy and education.

What kind of support is our society providing for them? As a young man, I taught English in that program for Vietnam veterans, so I got a sense of life after service is over, after physical wounds are healed, after the ceremonies—if there were any—and handshakes have receded into memory. Then soldiers have their lives to pick up or to create anew.

Advocates brought to public attention the inadequate funding and delivery of health care for recent vets; less public—until the deliberations surrounding the new G.I. Bill—were the limited resources for education and the many problems young veterans face as they try to reenter school. The rising cost of living combined with rising costs of tuition, textbooks, and supplies dash many hopes, but even those who can make it financially typically face significant academic and social problems.

The program that contained the communications class could serve as a model for how to help the men and women returning from Iraq and Afghanistan. Fortunately, a number of colleges are responding to this new generation of veterans with a range of support services: financial aid assistance, counseling, orientation programs, and social clubs. These are valuable resources. But my sense is that returning soldiers would be better served through a program that includes significant coursework as well as services. One such effort is the laudable SERV program at Cleveland State. But there are few others. The programs I'd like to see could run through some part of the first year or function as a preparatory or bridge program that precedes but is linked to further matriculation.

The key idea is to treat a complex educational issue in a comprehensive and integrated way. To respond adequately to academic needs, the program has to address psychological, social, and economic needs as well. And, hand in glove, some social and psychological problems—inability to concentrate, feelings of intellectual inadequacy—don't fully manifest themselves unless one is in a classroom, immersed in English or math or poli sci.

The Veterans Special Education Program was a twelve-week crash course in college preparation. The veterans called it academic boot camp. The curriculum included representative freshman-year courses in English, psychology, communications, and mathematics, so students got a sense of what lay before them— a reality check—and were able to begin college with some credits, a leg up. The courses also addressed fundamental cognitive and social skills: critical writing and reading, mathematics, human relations, and communication.

The courses were supported with tutoring. A number of the veterans had poor academic backgrounds, so some needed a good deal of assistance with their writing, with reading academic material, or with all the strategies for doing well in school: managing time, note taking, studying for exams. But the tutoring also made the academic work more humane, no small thing, for many of the students carried with them a history of insecurity and anger about matters academic.

They were being asked to write essays analyzing poetry or comparing sociological or psychological theories and to read more carefully and critically than they had before. The challenge stirred strong feeling. Some of the students shut down and withdrew, and others erupted. One marine scout I was working with got so frustrated that, in a blur of rage and laughter, he bit off the corner of his paper before handing it to me.

It wasn't enough for us to do our work within the confines of the classroom. The staff would follow up when a student missed a few days, making phone calls, driving over to an apartment or hotel room, finding someone in awful shape. We had a rich network of referrals for psychological counseling—the nearby VA hospitals but also local agencies and civic organizations. And for those who needed it, we had referrals for financial counseling as well. Finally, the program included assisting the students in selecting and applying to appropriate colleges and universities. With help from our counselor, the fellow who sank his teeth into that essay got into UCLA, majoring in sociology and East Asian studies.

All this created a sense of community, something the veterans often noted. For all their social and political differences, they shared the war, and now they were preparing for reentry into the world they left behind. The staff put on social events, but the real community, I believe, was formed through a course of study that was intensive, generous with assistance, and geared toward the next phase of the veterans' lives.

We have been awash with "support our troops" rhetoric, and politicians use it as a patriotic trump card. One grand irony in all this is the shameful level of health care some veterans have been getting and the resistance a number of conservatives and the Pentagon itself displayed in the face of legislation for a new G.I. Bill.

Rather than patriotic talk, I'd like to hear about programs that are comprehensive and address the multiple needs our troops have when they return home. Programs that provide knowledge and build skill. Programs that are thick with human contact. Programs that meet veterans where they are and provide structure and guidance that assist them toward a clear goal. Programs that build a community while leading these young men and women back to their own communities.

Educational programs for special populations tend toward single-shot solutions: a few basic skills courses, or tutoring, or counseling. But the best programs work on multiple levels, integrate a number of interventions. Such programs emerge from an understanding of the multiple barriers faced by their participants, but also from an affirmation of the potential of those participants. This is a huge point. The richness of the program matches the perception of the capacity of the people who populate it.

This is how really to support our troops. And it is how we should think about an education that, of necessity, has to go beyond the classroom.

TWELVE

The Inner Life of the Poor

THE POOR ARE PRETTY MUCH ABSENT from public and political discourse, except as an abstraction— an income category low on the socioeconomic status index—or as a generalization: people dependent on the government, the "takers," a problem. Neither abstraction nor generalization gives us actual people waking up exhausted, getting kids off to school; trying to make a buck; or, in some cases, past the point of trying. And if we lack images of living, breathing people, we doubly lack any sense of the inner lives of the poor. There are occasional journalistic profiles and some powerful urban ethnographies and fictional portrayals, but in general, the poor are invisible and silent. Because of the various layers of segregation in our society—from work to schools to places of worship—few of us have opportunities to live and work closely with people who are at the bottom of the income ladder. We don't know them. And because we don't know their values and aspirations, the particulars of their daily decisions, and the economic and psychological boundaries within which those decisions are made, they easily become psychologically one-dimensional, intellectually, emotionally, and volitionally simplified, not quite like us. This fact has huge implications for public policy, education and work, and civic life.

There are, of course, times when the poor burst into public life more fully formed: trapped miners are interviewed, a farmhand or day laborer rescues a child, a Fannie Lou Hamer or Cesar Chavez has had enough. "I am sick and tired," Hamer famously said, "of being sick and tired."

I've been interested in the psychological diminishment of poor people for a long time. My personal history as the son of working-class immigrant parents sensitizes me to it, and my teaching in low-income communities and my writing about education and social class has me thinking and thinking about it. Let me offer a portrait to get us closer inside this issue.

———

Joanie tended to my stepfather when he was in a board and care facility. He was cognitively impaired and could barely talk, but Joanie comprehended him and communicated with him. She had a really good way with him, fussed over him, and watched out for his safety with a hawk eye. But you might not get to see those qualities outside the facility. Joanie, a thirty-seven-year-old Mexican American, is a tough woman, walks with authority, dresses in loose sweats, T-shirts, windbreakers, and running shoes. She is wary and quick with invective if she feels wronged.

Ten years ago, she was taking classes at a community college and got a certificate in early childhood development, but soon found that she preferred working with the elderly. She enrolled in a for-profit occupational college and got a Certified Nursing Assistant (CNA) certificate, which put her in debt she's still paying off.

Around the time she was finishing that certificate, Joanie got into a fight with another woman over some guy, and the woman grabbed a broken bottle off the street and slashed deep into Joanie's right cheek. Joanie couldn't afford adequate medical care, and the wound didn't heal properly, leaving her with pain and sensitivity that continue to this day. Worse for Joanie was the disfigurement. She should just kill herself, a relative told her, for no man could love her. When I first met Joanie about five or six years after the injury, part of the right side of her face was darker and redder than her lustrous bronze skin. A birthmark, I thought.

Officially, there are close to two million home health care workers in the United States, and who knows how many more off the books. It is one of the fastest-growing occupations in the country. Most are female. Many are immigrants, particularly in larger cities, and there are significant numbers like Joanie, native born with varying levels of education. Their average wage is $9.70 per hour, and their annual income is $20,500. But the majority, like Joanie, do not have regular employment and move from one home or facility to another. It is hard work with limited, if any, benefits, and it is unsteady.

All the while I knew Joanie, she was dependable and upbeat, but it's only been in the last five or six months that she has slowly opened up about her life. It began when I started urging her to go back to school, to go to the community college she attended and get her records, so that we could see how far she was from an associate of arts degree. I'd pay for any cost. Her response was a mix of interest and reluctance: *It was so long ago. What would I do with those courses? It's such a hassle over there.* But she knew she needed to move beyond where she is now. *O.K. I'll do it. Yes.* Weeks would pass. More ambivalence. More resolves to go to the college.

This kind of paralysis is familiar to all of us as we try to break a habit, lose weight, or get out of a bad situation. But when poor people do it, we have a tendency to give it a particular gravity, to make it an explanation for why they are poor.

During this period, Joanie started talking to me about politics. Maybe all this talk about going back to school triggered such discussion. She drew on her own history but also on liberal and left-wing media, Jon Stewart to Pacifica Radio. I had known Joanie for years and had no inkling of her engagement with social issues.

I didn't let up on those transcripts. *You need more security, Joanie. Do you want to still be piecing together a living day by day when you're forty-five? You're smart and so skilled with old people.* She'd agree, seeming more resolved—but still no follow-through. What can seem so simple to those of us who have crossed a line in the social order or who have always been on the advantaged side of the line can be almost insurmountable for people like Joanie, not because of weak character or laziness or any other of the easy explanations we hear, but because of despair.

One day while I was watching Joanie play a board game with my stepfather, she turned to me and started crying, talking and crying. Her face hurt all the time, she said, and she was disfigured, and she'd never be able to fall in love. She knows she needs to get more education but doesn't know where . . . or how . . . or for what exactly. She has no money. She's on the outs with her family. She's treated like shit. "When you're shunned by society, it's awful. Nobody wants you." The pain and sadness poured out. I had pushed and pushed and tapped into deep hurt, a long history of trauma and assaults to the self that was intensified, embodied by her injury. She was both an outcast and physically unlovable. During the time I knew her, the damage to her face continued to resolve itself—the injury was barely visible—yet she still saw herself, felt herself, as scarred.

I won't go into detail about what I said to her and the various interventions I tried to help her find— except for one. A friend of mine was teaching a course at a local community college on Saturday mornings, and I put the two in touch and urged Joanie to attend. Joanie could walk to the campus.

It's a course for people who are coming back to school: a mix of advice, group counseling, and nitty-gritty help on navigating the system. For example, my friend would be able to access Joanie's earlier college records online and evaluate them for her. Joanie went. And went again the following week. She connected with the instructor. She made some acquaintances in the class. And she began to talk about having a "foot in the door" and finishing the college education she started so long ago. She wonders if she could become a social worker.

There's a lot that can go awry. Joanie might not be able to support herself, or might land a full-time job that makes school difficult. But what strikes me is how the simple act of walking onto that small campus twenty minutes from her house and signing up for a class that provided no graduation credit, how that action had such consequences for Joanie, disrupting years of forlorn paralysis. "You lose hope," she said. "You can't expect anything." But now there's a pitch to her voice that I haven't heard before. A life of hardship, a long history of insult and disappointment, wears you out, can clamp down the desire to be competent, to grow, to reach right beyond what you can currently do. That is what happens to a dream deferred. But when it suddenly seems possible to extend your reach, well, that's the fundamental experience of opportunity, and it can be liberating.

———

It shouldn't even need to be said that one can find among people with significantly limited financial and

material resources a wide array of thoughts and feelings. The content of those thoughts and feelings will
differ person by person and may well differ on average
from the thoughts and feelings of people who are financially secure—among the poor, there will be more
anxiety about basic health care and putting food on
the table. But in terms of the general architecture and
categories of thoughts and feelings, we share a common humanity: we all feel sadness and pleasure, try to
solve problems and make plans, take stock of what's in
front of us, find refuge in imagination.

While this claim may be psychologically true, it
is not at all a social or ideological given. Historian
Michael Katz has detailed the ways we in the United
States have stigmatized the poor through our definitions of them (for example, as undeserving or morally
weak) and through the policies we establish to provide
assistance to them, such as our narrow and punitive
welfare system. Appearance, race, language, and neighborhood are intimately involved in this construction
of the poor as different and inferior. The poor, writes
Katz are "strangers in our midst: Poor people think,
feel, and act in ways unlike middle-class Americans."
The label "the poor" itself becomes a categorical
term freighted with deficiency.

Part of the way we establish our shared humanity is by what we imagine goes on inside the head and the heart of others. If we are separated from a group not only physically but psychologically, then it becomes all the easier to attribute to them motives, beliefs, thoughts—an entire interior life—that might be deeply inaccurate and inadequate. And it is from those attributions that we develop both our personal and public policy responses to poverty.

Because the invisibility of the poor is ultimately a sociological and political phenomenon, I am interested in places or occasions where poor people become more fully present, actors on the societal stage, their thoughts and feelings playing out in ways that can have a positive effect on the direction of their lives. Social movements provide such a space. Cultural projects do as well—in churches and community centers, women's shelters, prison arts programs. And, in my experience, second-chance educational programs and institutions—literacy centers, adult schools, many community colleges—can also play this role. These are complex places, however; given the intricate relation in our country among social class, educational resources, and academic achievement, the adult school and community college reflect educational inequality and can contribute to it. A lot of students never complete a certificate or degree. But some institutions do better than others with similar populations, so the quality of governance, services, and teaching matters. These institutions are among the few places in mainstream society where poor people can become more publicly visible and display to their advantage multiple dimensions of their lives. As illustration, I'll draw on examples from one community college I've been studying over the past two years—in fact, it's the place where I directed Joanie.

Like many second-chance programs and schools, the college is a modest place, and it draws on one of the poorest populations in the region. As you begin to spend time on the campus and talk to people, one of the first things that strikes you is their raw desire to be involved and their pleasure at the opportunity. "I'm doing something better for myself," one woman says proudly. A man who never finished high school observes that "this is the first time school has meant anything to me." "From the first day on campus," a second-year student says, "I was in the zone, man. I loved it, and I'm still in love with it." I think of Zoe, a middle-aged woman I met during the first week of classes. She is lively and chatty but turns serious when she talks about the basic math course she has to take. This time, she says, she wants to learn math, really learn it. She waves her hand—blue nail polish, cigarette—across the campus. "I didn't know it would be this good," she says. "This is nice."

As students begin to invest in particular areas of study, this desire channels into occupational or academic fields. It's notable how often you'll hear the word "love" used, as in "I love welding." A fashion student quips, "I'd rather break my head on this than anything else." When I asked a young man what it is about physics that grabs him, he says he's captivated by "the wonder of it." As students get more courses under their belts and begin to acquire more substantial knowledge and skill, they develop a sense of competence and confidence, a kind of cognitive momentum that gets expressed both volitionally ("Nothing's going to stop me," the physics major says) and as intellectual curiosity and a desire for further mastery. After a field trip to a state-of-the-art welding shop, a student said he found all the new advances "overwhelming . . . there is so much more to know," but he adds quickly that the trip "motivated" him, for he "loves this stuff." "You will grow in a way," one woman muses, "that you never in your mind would imagine."

For some people, this return to school is intimately tied to existential goals. They talk of wanting to change their lives, to "do right by my kids," to

MIKE ROSE

"turn my life around," to "be somebody in this world." There is regret, reassessment, commitment. A man re-uniting with his wife and daughter after prison writes, "Now I have something to live for and someone living for me." What is fascinating is that, in some cases, this commitment begins with an epiphany, a lightbulb going on. The insight can hit in the flow of powerful events—a guy lands in jail for the umpteenth time, a loved one leaves you or dies, a seemingly stable job is torn away. It also can come while walking down the street or, as with one young woman, looking out across the retail store where she worked and imagining herself still there in ten years. People say things like, "What am I doing?" "What's my purpose in life?" "Why did God put me on this earth?"

The existential dimension of schooling is powerfully illustrated through Sam, a midtwenties African American man I've interviewed extensively. He was raised in foster care, bounced from one house to another, fathered a child at sixteen, got into trouble with the law, and spent several years in the criminal justice system. He eventually entered an occupational program at the college, got involved in student government, began tutoring on campus and working in a summer enrichment program for middle-school kids, and is now taking liberal arts courses and preparing to

transfer to a four-year college. The tutoring and summer work with middle schoolers has so engaged him
that he wants to teach or in some way work with people in need. There is much to say about the interior
life of this young man, but I'll focus on his ongoing
struggle to come to terms with a terribly impoverished
childhood. He has sought family surrogates for some
time, occasionally finding temporary solace with a relative, a girlfriend's family, teachers. "I've always wanted
to belong somewhere."

His yearning for deep connection is profound, and
as he has moved successfully through the college, this
yearning has blended healthily with his achievement as
a student, a tutor, and a member of student government: "It's like I have a big family, and I belong here."
Still, as his day draws to an end, and he heads for
home, memories and desires flood in: "all of my past
insecurities of feeling inferior or not feeling wanted
start to trickle in, and I become depressed and feel
like, 'Why do I have to still be alone?'" He attempts to
counter these feelings with cognitive-behavioral techniques that he found on the Internet. Two foundational questions consume him: how to be a man and
how to create a good and meaningful life.

Growing up on the streets and on the football
field—he was a standout athlete before his troubles

with the law—the definitions of manhood he absorbed are ones he rejects now. He is methodical and thoughtful as he fashions a new definition for himself, one that includes helping others, being respectful toward women, reuniting with his daughter ("Knowing that she's depending on me, I have to work hard"), having the ability to make and fix things (something his trade has afforded him), having an effect on the world. All of this—human connection, coming to terms with hurt and loss, growing into manhood, doing meaningful work, making a difference— reminds one of Freud's dictum about the key to the good life being love and work.

———————

I could write a companion essay on the inner horrors of poor people's lives—and we get a glimpse of those horrors in Joanie's story. Poverty wreaks terrible psychological damage— depression, fear, fury—and the result can range from withdrawal to violence to self and others. A number of the people whose lives are represented in this chapter grew up in—and, in some cases, still struggle against—this harsh psychological and social reality. But here I offer an account we hear much less frequently, a multidimensional story of motivation and intellectual engagement, of existential deliberation, of achievement that leads to the shaping of one's future.

How do we create the conditions in our institutions—or create new institutions entirely—that will enable more poor people to have the opportunities experienced by those we just met? I've been using the community college as an example, but what I'm going to write has relevance to other public institutions as well.

If they are truly *public*, then our institutions should be run with a deep knowledge of the motives, aspirations, cognitive capacity, and inner and outer barriers of the full range of the people they serve. In the case of the community college, such knowledge would affect the scheduling of classes and services, the distribution of financial aid and emergency loans, the provision of day care, the training of staff and faculty, the function of the library and the provision of Internet access, and more. Effective colleges are responding in this way. Some of these accommodations would require new resources, but others would involve a redistribution of current resources and, perhaps more important, a change in institutional vision.

A deep knowledge of poor people's lives would also lead to policy that connects institutions to each other, creating a network of assistance. Many students need help with food and shelter, or health care, or transportation. Their development is limited as well by the fraying of the social safety net. It is not uncommon that students have to take leave of their studies to support parents or siblings financially or help them during a health crisis.

But I think the fundamental thing that increased understanding of the inner lives of poor people could yield is a redefinition of certain public institutions themselves as places in an unequal social structure that address some of the injuries, both physical and psychic, wrought by that inequality. Again, I'll use the community college as an example.

It is instructive to look at the demands for change being made of the community college. It is an institution under scrutiny, and justifiably so, for its generally low rates of completion of certificates or degrees and for its poor record on transfer to four-year colleges and universities. There are calls to do something about the high percentage of students who are held for remediation in English or math by improving the quality of remedial instruction (a good thing) or by restricting enrollment of low-skilled students— a troubling alternative. There are also calls to amp up the academic side of the curriculum, emphasizing the transfer function, with a possible diminishment of occupational education. And some are questioning the modern mission of the community college itself as a comprehensive, open-door institution. The college is trying to be all things to all people, from providing enrichment classes to the general community to occupational courses for displaced workers to a lower-division education for those headed toward the baccalaureate. The community college cannot do all this well, the critics say, and therefore needs to trim and focus its efforts.

I agree with much of this criticism—we absolutely need to improve the quality of remediation and the rates of transfer—but I'm also reminded of something Michael Harrington said about discussions of poverty and inequality: "In America, we are always having the wrong debate." In the community college policy debates, we pit the comprehensive, open-door college against a leaner, meaner institution, or the academic function versus the vocational, or conceive of remediation as de facto antithetical to substantial education. What we should be talking about instead is the need to define the community college as an uniquely American institution that, at its best, can provide a public, mainstream, widely distributed institutional space—there are about 1,150 of them in the United States—where people with limited resources and opportunities can begin to direct their lives and find expression for their hopes and abilities.

The importance of the community college and other second-chance institutions is certainly recognized. More than a few of Barack Obama's speeches are delivered from community colleges, but the discussion of them is always in economic and functional terms. They are places where people will learn "twenty-first-century job skills." The courses mentioned, always and unerringly, are technical ones: science, math, engineering, and the occupational offspring of them. There is nothing wrong with an economic, practical focus. The people attending these courses—just like the people we've heard from in this chapter—desperately want to better their economic prospects. The problem is that both policy deliberation and political rhetoric stop there.

I have yet to find in political speech or policy documents any significant discussion of what benefit—other than economic—the community college might bring. There is no talk of literature or the arts, of political science and sociology, of world culture—nothing beyond the technical. There is no discussion of the kinds of intellectual growth and reflection we witnessed at the college I visited, no sense that the education the students are receiving—from English and physics to nursing and welding—sparks emotion, aesthetic response, reassessments of one's ability and identity.

Our era's technocratic tunnel vision is in play here, but I believe something else is going on as well, and that is the pinched understanding of the inner lives of poor people. The intersection of a reductive, technocratic orientation with the aura of deficiency that surrounds the poor not only dehumanizes our public institutions but makes them less effective. To have a prayer of achieving a society that realizes the potential of all its citizens, we will need institutions that affirm the full humanity, the wide sweep of desire and ability of the people walking through the door.

THIRTEEN

Finding the Public Good Through the Details of Classroom Life

So MUCH DEPENDS on what you look for and how you look for it. In the midst of the reform debates and culture wars that swirl around schools; the fractious, intractable school politics; the conservative assault on public institutions; and the testing, testing, testing— in the midst of all this, it is easy to lose sight of the broader purpose of the common public school. For me, that purpose is manifest in the everyday detail of classrooms, the words and gestures of a good teacher, the looks on the faces of students thinking their way through a problem.

We have so little of such detail in our national discussion of teaching, learning, or the very notion of public education itself. It has all become a contentious abstraction. But detail gives us the sense of a place, something that can get lost in policy discussions about our schools—or, for that matter, in so much of our national discussion about ourselves. Too often, we deal in broad brushstrokes about regions, about politics and economics, about racial, linguistic, and other social characteristics. Witness the red state–blue state distinction, one that, yes, tells us something quick and consequential about averages, but misses so much about local social and political dynamics, the lived civic variability within.

The details of classroom life convey, in a specific and physical way, the intellectual work being done day to day across the nation—the feel and clatter of teaching and learning. I'm thinking right now of a scene in a chemistry class in Pasadena, California, that I observed. The students had been conducting experiments to determine the polarity of various materials. Some were washing test tubes, holding them up to the windows for the glint of sunlight, checking for a bad rinse. Some were mixing salt and water to prepare one of their polar materials. Some were cautiously filling droppers with hydrochloric acid or carbon tetrachloride. And some were stirring solutions with glass rods, squinting to see the results. There was lots of chatter and lots of questions for the teacher, who walked from student to student, asking what they were doing and why, and what they were finding out.

The students were learning about the important concept of polarity. They were also learning to be systematic and methodical. And moving through the room was the teacher, asking questions, responding, fostering a scientific cast of mind. This sort of class-room scene is not uncommon. And collectively, such moments give a palpable sense of what it means to have, distributed across a nation, available by law to all, a public educational system to provide the opportunity for such intellectual development.

Citizens in a democracy must continually assess the performance of their public institutions. But the quality and language of that evaluation matter. Before we can evaluate, we need to be clear about what it is we're evaluating, what the nature of the thing is: its components and intricacies, its goals and purpose. We should also ask why we're evaluating. To what end?

Neither the sweeping rhetoric of public school failure nor the narrow focus on test scores helps us here. Both exclude the important, challenging work done daily in schools across the country, thereby limiting the educational vocabulary and imagery available to us. This way of talking about schools constrains the way we frame problems and blinkers our imagination. "We can all agree," wrote a contributing editor for the *Weekly*

Standard not long ago, "that American public schools are a joke." Such a statement doesn't even leave us with a problem to solve.

There have been times in our history when the idea of "the public" has been invested with great agency and hope. Such is not the case now. An entire generation has come of age amid disillusionment with public institutions and public life, disillusionment born of high-profile government scandal and institutional inefficiency, but, even more, from a skillful advocacy by conservative policy makers and pundits of the broad virtues of free markets and individual enterprise.

Clearly, there are domains of public life that benefit from market forces, and individual enterprise is a powerful force for both personal advancement and public benefit. Moreover, the very notion of "public" is a fluid one; it changes historically, exists in varied relationships to the private sector, and, on occasion, fuses with that sector in creative ways. And, as I have noted, we must not simply accept our public institutions as they are, but be vigilantly engaged with them.

Our reigning orthodoxy on the public sphere, however, is much less nuanced. Though the financial crisis of late 2008 led to a momentary questioning of market virtues, we are once again celebrating the market and private initiative as the answers to our social and civic obligations. This orthodoxy downplays, often dismisses, the many ways that markets need to be modified to protect common people and the common good against market excesses—for markets are relentlessly opportunistic and dollar driven.

The orthodoxy operates with a heavy dose of social amnesia, erasing the history of horrible market failure and of private greed that led to curbs on markets and the creation of robust public institutions and protections. The free-market believers' infatuation slides quickly to blithe arrogance about all things public. A man is being interviewed on National Public Radio. "The post office," he says, "is the worst-run business in America." This was within the same week as the opening of the trial of Enron's Jeffrey Skilling and Kenneth Lay on multiple fraud charges, and we have had numerous examples of corporate wrongdoing since.

The easy dismissiveness of the public sector also has its ugly side, characterizing anything public as inferior . . . or worse. I remember a Los Angeles talk-show host who called the children enrolled in the Los Angeles school district "garbage." And, in a comment both telling and sad, the kids I meet in schools have said on several occasions that they know people think of them as "debris" or "trash."

We have to do better than this. We have to develop

a revitalized sense of public life and public education. One tangible resource for such a revitalization comes for me out of the thousands of small, daily events of classroom life I have witnessed.

This sense of the possible emerges when a child learns to take another child seriously, learns to think something through with other children, learns about perspective and the range of human experience and talent. It comes when, over time, a child arrives at an understanding of numbers, or acquires skill in rendering an idea in written language. It is there when a group of students crowd around a lab table trying to figure out why a predicted reaction fizzled. When a local event or regional dialect or familiar tall tale becomes a creative resource for visual art or spoken word. When a developing athlete plants the pole squarely in the box and vaults skyward. When a student says that his teacher "coaxes our thinking along." When a teacher, thinking back on it all, muses on the power of "watching your students at such an important time in their lives encounter the world."

It is in such moments—moments in public school classrooms—that something of immense promise for the nation is being confirmed.

There is, of course, nothing inherently public or private about such activities. They occur daily in private schools, in church organizations, in backyards. But there is something compelling, I think, about raising one's gaze outward, beyond the immediate doorway or fence, to the biology lesson at the forest's edge or the novel crammed into the hip pocket in the center of the city. The public school gives rise to these moments in a common space, supports them, commits to them as a public good, affirms the capacity of all of us, contributes to what the post–Revolutionary War writer Samuel Harrison Smith called the "general diffusion of knowledge" across the republic. Such a mass public endeavor creates a citizenry.

As our notion of the public shrinks, the full meaning of public education, the cognitive and social luxuriance of it, fades. Achievement is still possible, but loses its civic heart.

The Journey Back and Forward

THERE WERE FOUR WIDE BOARDS nailed to the front wall of the Little Greenbrier Schoolhouse, an empty one-room school off Highway 321, between Townsend and Greeneville, Tennessee. The boards were painted black, a chalkboard. The desks were separated into four columns, seven rows deep; there was a long bench in front. I imagined the youngest children sitting there. Then, arranged by age, the others, probably through eighth grade, found their desks. It was dark but for the glow of daylight that filled the open door and window; thin streaks of sunlight pierced through the gaps in the walls. I walked to the last row—the floor creaking—and sat down, picturing a column of numbers on the blackboard, hearing the rough tap of chalk.

I found the Greenbrier School during one of my trips across the United States trying to gain, in one irregular arc, some sense of the sweep and scope of this country. Schools were much on my mind, education everywhere in the landscape. Schools are nested in place—for all their regularity, they reflect local history, language, and cultural practices. Before long, classrooms and terrain began to play off each other. A science lesson led to the creek beyond the window; a sonnet broke its line to the honking of horns. The often-maligned intelligence of the nation seemed at these moments as rich and layered as its variegated landscape.

I visited one-room schoolhouses at more than a few points in the journey. Some were abandoned. And some were still in full operation. The empty ones, though, caught my fancy, and got me to thinking about their origins, and the origins of the common school.

Depending on era and region, the schoolhouses were built of sod, adobe, or logs, stone or clapboard. By and large, they were harsh, uncomfortable places. School life met the demands of the farm calendar, with some schools open for seven or eight months, some for three or four. A plaque on the Greenbrier Schoolhouse noted that some children went for six weeks. The one-room school typically included first through eighth grades; ages and attendance varied widely, and class size ranged from half a dozen to forty or more. For all their variety, and given the minimal centralized regulation—they epitomized local control—they were surprisingly uniform in their organization (young children in front, older in back), pedagogy (heavy on memorization, drill, and recitation), and curriculum: reading, writing (grammar, spelling, penmanship), arithmetic, U.S. history, physiology, geography.

Standing alone before one of these empty schools, I would wonder about the children who once gathered there. The teacher walks to the door, about to call them in for the morning. She's young, works for one-third less pay than a man, most likely has a high school education or less, perhaps barely out of country school herself. If she's not local, she boards with one of the families of her pupils or lives in a small, minimally appointed teacherage, open to the scrutiny of the community. Her letters may well reflect what many from the time reflect: the loneliness and vulnerability, the frustration over discipline and inadequate supplies, the challenge of so many lessons, all those kids. Still, the work offered one of the few avenues to independence and authority. It was a chance, as one young woman put it, to "try myself alone and find out what I am."

At the turn of the twentieth century, there were

more than 200,000 functioning one-room school-houses in the United States; now there are fewer than 400 spread throughout the states, with the largest numbers located in Montana and Nebraska. Population shifts and continued pressure toward consolidation led to the closing of the one-room school. Now, we look back on them with a mix of nostalgia and curiosity, surprised, perhaps, that some still exist.

Those old schools could be violent and stultifying places; the writer Hamlin Garland called the one he attended "a barren temple of the arts." And teaching in them was tough duty. Yet it is also true—and we are not good at tolerating the ambiguity—that this wildly uneven array of schools contributed profoundly to the literacy and numeracy of the nation. Out of local effort and varied conditions emerged the common good.

I look at these old schoolhouses, so distant, yet what they represent is very much with us, topics that are woven throughout *Why School?*: how to educate a vast population, how to bring schooling to all, what to teach and how to teach it, who will do it, what the work will mean to them—what we can help make it mean to them.

We still ask these questions because we haven't satisfactorily answered them. We have such a troubled history, for example, educating children of the working class. But we ask the questions as well because a neat and final answer is not possible or desirable in an open society. We honor these questions best by revisiting them. And the way we answer them says a lot about who we are—and what we want to become.

From the beginning we have invested great hope in the common school—consider Jefferson's vision of it as central to democratic life. And from the beginning we have expected our schools to teach more than skills and subject matter, notably a sense of civic duty and moral behavior. These extrascholastic expectations have increased dramatically. I found in one schoolhouse documents from the early twentieth century recording that instruction was given on "the effects of alcoholic drinks and narcotics" and on "the prevention of communicable diseases."

Throughout the twentieth century and into our time, the public as well as school administrators and reformers have turned to the public school, especially the high school, to address the many needs of young people that may once have been met by families, churches, employers, and volunteer groups: from hygiene to job preparation. We also resort to the public schools to solve the broad social and economic problems that we cannot or will not adequately address by other means. One of the purposes of school desegregation, for example, was to disrupt residential patterns resulting from racism, demographic shifts, and housing policy. And we continue to look to the schools to address the effects of deindustrialization, immigration, chronic poverty—and now an increasingly globalized economy.

It is entirely reasonable that a society will turn to its basic institutions to solve pressing needs. My concern, evident throughout this book, is that the economic motive and the attendant machinery of standardized testing has overwhelmed all the other reasons we historically have sent our children to school. Hand in glove, this motive and machinery narrow our sense of what school can be. We hear much talk about achievement and the achievement gap, about equity, about increasing effort and expectations, but it is primarily technical and organizational talk, thin on the ethical, social, and imaginative dimensions of human experience.

If we abstract out of education policy a profile of the American student during the early decades of the twenty-first century it would be this: a young person being prepared for the world of work, measured regularly, trained to demonstrate on a particular kind of test a particular kind of knowledge. This is not Jefferson's citizen-in-the-making. And in my experience most parents of a wide range of backgrounds and political persuasions, though they want their children to develop basic skills and be prepared for work, want much more.

In *Democracy and Education* John Dewey offers this celebratory snapshot of a child's mind in action:

> The child of three who discovers what can be done with blocks, or of six who finds out what he can make by putting five cents and five cents together, is really a discoverer, even though everybody else in the world knows it.

There is a rendering of cognitive growth here that is familiar to primary school teachers and is cherished by parents, yet we'd be hard pressed to find this sort of wonder in contemporary education policy. Think, too, how little we hear about the majesty of intelligence—and this in an age of astounding feats of mind, from the landing of a robotic explorer on Mars to the probing of human consciousness itself. As for creativity, it rarely makes an appearance in lists of core competencies. If this state of affairs is true for policy involving K–12, it is doubly true for postsecondary and adult education.

There is little talk of the power of teaching, of this

remarkable kind of human relationship, honored in all cultures. In our time, teaching is acknowledged as important but is often defined as a knowledge-delivery system. Yet teaching carries with it the obligation to understand the people in one's charge, to teach subject matter and skills, but also to inquire, to nurture, to have a sense of who a student is. Parents mention these qualities all the time, and they are often what draw students to the intellectual content of science, literature, or history, and to the very idea of school as a good place to be.

Our major policy documents contain little mention of the obligations of government to its citizens, of protections against inequality, of a comprehensive notion of educational opportunity. No surprise, then, that we do not find a robust discussion of the notion of the public or of the democratic citizen—that portrayal of the citizen not just as an economic being, but as a deliberative, civic, moral being as well. We are a society with a system of mass education, but to what degree can we define ourselves as an educated society?

How we think about and voice the purpose of school matters. It affects what we put in or take out of the curriculum and how we teach that curriculum.

It affects the way we think about students—all students—about intelligence, achievement, human development, teaching and learning, opportunity and obligation. And all of this affects the way we think about each other and who we are as a nation.

AFTERWORD

Writing About School

To write about education is to write about the human condition. It means you're writing about people learning and growing, or running up against their limits, or being thwarted by forces and events beyond their control. The writing, then, is about possibility, challenge, disappointment, failure, meaning, identity.

To write about education is to write about institutions and institutional behavior: traditions and bureaucracy and battles over turf—and the way savvy teachers and administrators and counselors learn to navigate all that. And the institutional wisdom they display in itself makes for quite a story.

To write about education is also to write about social attitudes and beliefs, for schools are porous institutions and what is outside their walls manifests within those walls. And to write about education is to write about politics and economics, both of which affect schools profoundly.

219

And finally, to write about education is to write about our society's definition of itself, our guiding principles. This takes us into history, and that history is replete with injustice and violations of ideals as well as the realization of democracy and human potential.

It's this scope and sweep—from the details of a classroom to national vision—that helps explain the power and pleasure of writing about education.

I've taught and studied writing for over forty years, and during my time at the UCLA Graduate School of Education and Information Studies, I've developed two courses for our students: one to aid them in becoming better scholarly writers, and one to help them write about their work for general audiences. So much scholarly writing is tangled and opaque. I try in every way I can to get my students to see that writing well matters a lot—and I think they know, we all know, this intuitively. We know how a careful argument, a well-turned phrase, a respectful appeal captures our attention, even in the maddening flow of words across our screens.

In producing this Afterword, I thought back over my own writing, the writing I've appreciated during my time in education, and the work I've done in those writing classes. I condensed my advice down to twelve observations. I should note that I'm not only concerned about getting words on paper or on a screen. Since I think of writing as both analytical method and creative craft, a number of these observations include activities that both precede writing and enhance the writing itself.

1. Pay Attention to the Obvious

We all have spent so many years in school that it's hard for us to get any distance from it, to see it new, to, as the anthropologist suggests, "make it strange." And, paradoxically, one way to "make strange" is to record the obvious. Write down or sketch or take pictures of the most humdrum, everyday things:

- What surrounds the campus?
- Describe people entering the campus: on foot, on bicycles, in cars.
- How are desks arranged in a classroom? Sketch it.
- What kinds of questions does the teacher ask?
- How do students respond?
- How do students interact with each other?
- What does the teacher do physically: where does she stand, does she move through the room, what are her gestures?

My statistician colleague, Mike Seltzer, tells his students to do something similar before applying all their heavy technical machinery: Look closely at plots of data. Examine outliers. Summarize for yourself what you see.

This everyday material becomes so useful when you're trying to set a scene or explain context. And sometimes the mundane contains revelations—as when I realized after a few hours at a community college serving a quite poor section of the city how many people walked with some sort of a limp. I was at the college to study barriers to achievement, and this emerging observation about people's gait spoke volumes about trauma and health care.

2. The Value of Detail

I try to open up all my sensory antennae when I'm in a place I'm going to write about: The acrid smell of electrical heat in a factory, the bleats and blasts of instruments from the music room, the creak of old floors, the feeling of being jostled in a packed hallway. Detail makes writing come alive. But here's the thing about detail: you can get lost in details, whether they're verbal images or a slew of statistical correlations. So the details need to lead to an idea. The idea emerges from the detail and the detail grounds the idea.

3. Real Speech

We put a lot of stock in the formal interview or focus group. And both are valuable sources of information. But I prefer, when possible, to talk to people while they're doing something related to the topic of the interview. So, for example, I prefer to talk to the student nurse while she's practicing on a mannequin her technique for inserting an IV or with a teacher as soon as class is over. You're in the flow of their activity, and what they say will be more grounded, less of an abstraction or a surmise.

I also believe in keeping your ears open all the time, on the bus, the street, walking across campus. Never be without a small notepad. Attune your ears to the rhythms of speech, to the staccato give-and-take at a diner, to the fragments of a cell phone conversation. And sometimes the most casual conversation will present a phrase or sentence that captures perfectly the issues you're writing about, as when a student said to me as I was walking her to the bus, "You know, it's a terrible thing to not have any money."

4. A Story Needs to Do Something

Many of the stories people tell in everyday life have a moral to them, a point to make. Here's the basic plot-line: "If you act this way, do something this foolish or this brave or this considerate, then this is what's going to happen." I think a story in the writing we produce likewise has to do something. It needs to contain or build toward a claim or an argument of some kind. We are basically saying to the reader: Look, I'm telling you this story because I want to illustrate a point, or shine a new light on something, or reveal layers and tensions where we thought none existed. No matter how moving a story might be, it has work to do.

5. Numbers Tell a Story, Too

When I'm working with students who are doing a quantitative study, I ask them what story the numbers tell. That is, I want them to think about numbers narratively, for even a list or a table can tell a story. What is that story, and are you mindful of how you are telling that story to a reader? As your potential reader changes, for example, from someone who shares your knowledge to the broader public, how will you change the way you tell your story?

6. Using Personal Stories

Like a fair number of people these days, I use personal material in my speeches and writing. It can be from my teaching or from my experience running programs, but even closer to home, it can come from my own family history. There are legitimate arguments against using such material, but as some feminist social scientists would argue, personal history can provide a valuable way of knowing. Given my working-class upbringing, I understand things about social stratification that all the reading in the world couldn't provide. Or I have a sense of the complicated and contradictory set of attitudes someone like my mother—who worked as a waitress all her life—could have toward hard physical work.

I find great value, as well, in combining personal material with research, each benefiting the other. For example, as I was reading historian David Montgomery's extraordinary chapter on "The Common Laborer" (in *The Fall of the House of Labor*), I kept thinking of my grandfather, Tony Meraglio, who emigrated from Southern Italy to work in the Pennsylvania Railroad. As vivid as Montgomery's writing is, my knowledge of Tony—the stories I heard, the photograph on my desk—all brought a further depth of understanding to the historian's portrayal. Conversely, the context Montgomery provides, the macroview of social and economic forces, brings Tony to fuller life. He's not only a cluster of family stories but a man located in a time and a place. The table of labor statistics and the narrative of a life are quite different ways of representing the world, but they also can complement and enhance each other.

7. Be Skeptical of the Big Idea, the Hot Theory

I'm not a flat-earther or a climate change denier. I'm okay with theories. But when it comes to explanations of human behavior, I've found it helpful to push the pause button and think things through. We live in a TED-Talk universe, a time of remarkable transformations that give rise to big predictions and grand theories. But sometimes, human variability, nuance, the particularity of experience get lost in the excitement. I guess I have a hesitation about abstraction. No matter how captivating the idea or theory, I like to go slow, to be conservative, cautious. I want to test the ideas against what I know and my experience. If this idea is true, I ask myself, how would it manifest itself when people work in a group, or write a story, or raise children? I look for counter cases, disconfirming evidence. Is there an alternative explanation for what people are claiming? I might well end up buying the new idea, the big theory, but do so on more solid ground.

8. Testing an Idea with the Community in Your Head

Another way I like to test out an idea is to imagine different people I respect hearing or reading it. Now, let me be clear, I am *not* talking about all those nattering voices in your head that tell you that your writing stinks and that you're a dummy. No. For me, my auditors are people with a smart and distinct point of view—like my dissertation chair Rich Shavelson, a first-class applied statistician and research methodologist. Another might be my Uncle Joe, a guy who never finished high school, worked at General Motors all his life, and had a keen nose for bullshit. What would they say? And how can I incorporate what they say? Or argue back? Now, here's an important caveat: don't do this too early—don't *ever* do it when you're still generating ideas and words, for it can paralyze you. But once you've got something together, open the door and invite these imaginary readers into the room.

9. Take a Risk

Schools are complex, fascinating places, and to render that richness in writing, we sometimes need to move beyond standard story lines (for example, the struggling school), stock characters (the tough-love principal, the sullen student), and conventional style and form. We need to experiment, take a writerly risk. But because we're writing about real people in real places, we also have to be responsible to them, honor them. So I'm not talking here about throwing caution to the winds, nor advocating daredevil "look ma, no hands" risks. But creative intellectual risks. Let me pose the concept of *diligent risk*. There are certain protections and safeguards that can't be broken, certain demands of analytical rigor. But within these constraints interesting things can happen.

Let me give you an example from the genesis of my book *Lives on the Boundary*. Way before I entered my doctoral program in education, I had been writing poetry, some of it portraits of my family and other Italian immigrants from their era.

When in the late 1970s, I started writing academic essays and research articles, I continued the poetry, and these different kinds of writing, poetry and the academic essay, overlapped—but did not intersect in any way. Eventually, I became curious about the possibility of combining the writing I was doing. Scholarship and research gave me a set of powerful analytic tools, and I worked hard to get better at using them. And the poetry provided a medium to convert all the little pieces of daily life—from my grandmother's shawl to an old radio—into written language, and with that conversion came the development of descriptive skill. I didn't want to lose any of this. And I began to wonder: could analytic prose be blended with poetry?

So one day, and I still remember this vividly, I photocopied a few paragraphs on the structure of long-term memory from a cognitive psychology textbook and taped them on a large sheet of white paper. Underneath them, I placed some of those immigrant portraits. So I ended up with a discussion of memory processes right next to a depiction of memories. Why not? It was this sort of fooling around with text and genre that would lead to the form of *Lives on the Boundary*, which blends narrative with analysis.

Now, I'm not asking you to do quirky things with Scotch tape and butcher paper, but I firmly do believe that within the confines of our writing—and this includes everything from the course assignment to the policy brief to the newspaper opinion piece—there are possibilities, degrees of freedom, if you will, that we don't initially see, and that could enable us to write better, to communicate more effectively and power-fully about education in America.

10. Read Deep into the Grain and Read Grain Against Different Grain

We've all heard the phrase "to read against the grain," that is, to go beyond the easy interpretation, to read critically. This is absolutely a good thing to do. But let me offer two other approaches, using the wood-grain metaphor.

One I'll call reading deep into the grain, and by this I mean reading the history of what you're study-ing, regardless of what it is, from children learning to read to financial aid. I promise you that history will not only broaden your background understanding of something—its origins and other possible approaches or solutions that might have emerged—but also sharpen your analytic vision in the moment. I'm convinced that my reading about the history of the development of hand tools while observing a wood construction class helped me consider more carefully the learning I was trying to capture, even just a novice's refinement in the grip of a chisel or the swing of a hammer.

By reading grain against grain, I'm asking you to

read side-by-side material that is unexpected, that doesn't automatically match, combining cedar and oak. If you're writing about financial aid, read something in the anthropological literature on the practice of lending. Or if you're interested in current educational reform movements, skim through a book like Howard Segal's study of technological utopianism in American culture, for it will help you understand the faith we as a people place in technocratic solutions to social problems.

11. Dealing with Conflicting or Contradictory Information

Sometimes data come out screwy because we made a mistake in our analysis, or the elements in someone's story don't add up because we missed something or didn't ask the right questions. Back to the drawing board. But realize that sometimes things come out confusing and contradictory because, in fact, they *are* confusing and contradictory. Things are rarely simple when it comes to studying human behavior. Your job then is to render as best you can with numbers or stories or both that complicated reality. Don't try to smooth it out neatly to fit a claim or a seamless narrative or to force a main effect. The real treasure might rest in the conflicting findings, the messy tension.

12. Failure

Be ready to fail. Or, at the least, get ready to think you're failing. If you're doing something worthwhile, something that pushes on the edges of things even just a little, you're going to slam up against your limits, not to mention your insecurities and demons. Every large project of mine has had me waking up in the middle of the night convinced that I couldn't do it. When I was getting close to the end of *Possible Lives,* a chronicle of my travels across the United States visiting good public school classrooms, I had that dark night of the soul. Several of them. Wide awake at three or four in the morning, convinced I wasn't smart enough or skilled enough to know how to bring the book to a satisfying conclusion. How could I tell all those wonderful teachers I visited that I was going to let them down, was not able to tell their stories? What made me think I could do this project in the first place? Oh Lord, the humiliation! My God, the public shame!

Sound familiar?

Get out of bed. Get a drink of water. If you pray, then pray. If you take a pill, do that. Scribble some notes, if that helps. But realize that the odds are that you'll get through this, maybe with a new insight, maybe with a new way to frame the problem. I keep a little voice recorder by my bed just in case. Eventually, you'll get to the place where you're able to say to those little furry-footed demons: Oh, it's *you* again. Ask them if they'd like a drink . . . or one of those pills. Invite them to curl up at the foot of the bed. And then say a few words into your voice recorder.

ACKNOWLEDGMENTS

FOR HELP WITH THE SECOND EDITION, I want to thank Alison Bailey, Eva Baker, Liza Bolitzer, Sibyll Carnochan Catalan, Lisa Dillman, Marcy Drummond, Elyse Eidman-Aadahl, Pat Ford, Jan Frodesen, Joanna Goode, Kris Gutierrez, Casandra Harper, Michael Hendrickson, Jenn Ho, Joann Isken, Sarah Jean Johnson, Michael Katz, Elham Kazemi, Tatiana Melguizo, Rashmita Mistry, Ted Mitchell, Vicki Park, Jordan Rickles, Jon Schweig, Janelle Scott, Richard Shavelson, Molly Shea, Deborah Stipek, Tina Trujillo, Shirin Vossoughi, Tara Watford, Noreen Webb, and David Yeager. Each of these exceptionally talented people provided expertise and wisdom that made this new edition possible.

I also want to thank Megan Franke, Debbie Grodzicki, Patty Quinones, and Glory Tobiason for helping me track down elusive sources—and special thanks to Alejandra Priede-Schubert for extra assistance at the end. Cherie Nguyen and Elaine Thai prepared the manuscript through endless revisions and helped with research as well.

Jed Bickman was my editor for this edition, and I want to acknowledge his skill and consummate patience. Maury Botton masterfully guided the book through production. And, as with my other books with The New Press, Diane Wachtell's editorial magic made it all happen.

8   "Opportunity . . . dictionary definition": *American Heritage College Dictionary*, 3rd edition (Boston: Houghton Mifflin, 1993), 958.

11   "income rose 136 percent": "The Rich, the Poor and the Growing Gap Between Them," *The Economist* (June 17–23, 2006), 28–30.

12   "By 2010, a shocking 22 percent of children under eighteen were poor.": "Poverty in the United States: Frequently Asked Questions," National Poverty Center, Gerald R. Ford School of Public Policy, University of Michigan, 2013.

12   "Income inequality is growing": "Ever Higher Society, Ever Harder to Ascend," *The Economist* (January 1, 2005), 22–24, 22.

13   Horace Mann, "Fifth Report, for 1841," in *Life and Works of Horace Mann*, vol. 3, *Annual Reports of the Secretary of the Board of Education of Massachusetts for the Years 1839–1844* (Boston: Lee and Shepard Publishers, 1867; repr. 1891), 92–128.

15 "described my time with Mr. McFarland elsewhere": *Lives on the Boundary* (New York: Free Press, 1989/ Penguin, 1990).

30 "wealthiest public schools spend two to three times": Lawrence Picus, personal communication, August 15, 2005.

48 Robert Linn, "Assessments and Accountability," *Educational Researcher* (March 2000), 4–16, 14.

49 The National Academies Board on Testing and Assessment, http://www.nap.edu/openbook.php?record_id=12780&page=10.

49 "research shows this is happening": see, for example, Heinrich Mintrop and Tina Trujillo, "The Practical Relevance of Accountability Systems for School Improvement: A Descriptive Analysis of California Schools," *Educational Evaluation and Policy Analysis* 29, n. 4 (December 2007) 319–352.

52 "Fortunately for the reformers . . ." To get a sense of the complications involved in these kinds of studies, see Andrew J. Wayne and Peter Youngs, "Teacher Characteristics and Student Achievement Gains: A Review," *Review of Educational Research* 73, n. 1 (spring 2003), 89–122.

54 Margaret Spellings, "U.S. Secretary of Education Margaret Spellings Joins Former Governor Jeb Bush for National Summit on Education Reform," http://www.ed.gov/news/pressreleases/2008/06/06192008.html.

60 "a number of analysts": see, for example, William Peterson and Richard Rothstein, "Let's Do the Numbers: Department of Education's 'Race to the Top' Program Offers Only A Muddled Path to the Finish Line," Economic Policy Institute, Briefing Paper #263, April 20, 2010.

61 Tina Trujillo, personal communication, April 21, 2013.

65 "Secretary Duncan has said he would like to see this approach": ibid., 8.

68 Michael B. Katz, *The Price of Citizenship: Redefining the American Welfare State* (New York: Metropolitan Books, 2001), 356.

70 Raymond Callahan, *Education and the Cult of Efficiency: A Study of the Social Forces That Have Shaped the Administration of the Public Schools* (Chicago: University of Chicago Press, 1962).

72 Arne Duncan, "The New Normal: Doing More with Less," speech given at The American Enterprise Institute, November 17, 2012.

74 "Impact 15," *Forbes*, November 19, 2012.

77 Janelle Scott, personal communication, September 13, 2008.

83 Howard Gardner, *Frames of Mind: The Theory of Multiple Intelligences* (New York: Basic Books, 1983); Robert Sternberg, et al., *Practical Intelligence in Everyday Life* (Cambridge: Cambridge University Press, 2000).

85 "But work of the Industrial Age": Sandra Burud

and Marie Tumolo, *Leveraging the New Human Capital* (Mountain View, CA: Davies-Black Publishing, 2004), 33.

93 Theodore Lewis, "Vocational Education as General Education," *Curriculum Inquiry* 28, no. 3 (1998): 283–309, 291.

94 Glynda Hull, "What's in a Label?: Complicating Notions of the Skills-Poor Worker," *Written Communication* 16, n. 4 (1999): 379–411.

107 Paul Tough, *How Children Succeed: Grit, Curiosity, and the Hidden Power of Character* (New York: Houghton Mifflin, 2012). The names of people and programs involved in contemporary character education are drawn from Tough's book.

114 Boston School Committee: quoted in Michael B. Katz, *The Irony of Early School Reform* (Cambridge, Mass., Harvard University Press, 1968), 120.

118 Mina Shaughnessy, "Diving In: An Introduction to Basic Writing," *College Composition and Communication*, 27 (October 1976): 234–239.

126 Professor X, "In the Basement of the Ivory Tower," *Atlantic Monthly* (June 2008), 68–73.

128 James Joyce, "Araby," *Dubliners* (1916, New York: Viking, 1958), 29–35.

131 Manuel Luis Espinoza: http://mikerosebooks .blogspot.com/2008/06/on-portraying-non -traditional-college.html (from the "Anonymous" response to the blog on June 9, 2008).

133 John Dewey, *Democracy and Education* (1916, New York: The Free Press, 1966), 182–183.

140 Anthony Carnevale, quoted in Dana Goldstein, "The Schoolmaster," *The Atlantic*, September 20, 2012, 2.

141 "There are good reasons to worry": two useful sources here are Grant Wiggins's blog "Granted, and . . . thoughts on education," http://grantwiggins .wordpress.com/; and The Gordon Commission on the Future of Assessment in Education, *To Access, To Teach, To Learn: A Vision for the Future of Assessment*, http:// www.cse.ucla.edu/colloquium/GC_Report030513 _Report.pdf.

150 Daphne Kohler, "What We're Learning from On-line Education," TED video (filmed June 2012, posted August 2012), http://www.ted.com/talks/ daphne_koller_what_we_re_learning_from_online _education.html.

151 "tsunami": Ken Auletta, "Get Rich U," *The New Yorker*, April 30, 2012.

151 "avalanche": Michael Barber, Katelyn Donnelly, and Saad Rizvi, "An Avalanche Is Coming: Higher Education and the Revolution Ahead" (London: Institute for Public Policy Research, 2013).

151 "Napster moment": Clay Shirky, "Napster, Udacity, and the Academy," 2012, http://www.shirky .com/weblog/2012/11/napster-udacity-and-the -academy/.

152 "Some of the stronger critiques of MOOCs": see,

for example, Mark Guzdial's "Computing Education Blog," http://computinged.wordpress.com/.

157 William Bowen, *Higher Education in the Digital Age* (Princeton: Princeton University Press, 2013). Two (of many) other helpful sources are Andrew Delbanco, "MOOCs of Hazard," *New Republic*, March 31, 2013, http://www.newrepublic.com/article/112731/moocs-will-online-education-ruin-university-experience; and "Open Letter to Professor Michael Sandel from the Philosophy Department of San Jose State U," April 29, 2013, http://ubi-learn.com/the-latest-news/an-open-letter-to-professor-michael-sandel-from-the-philosophy-department-a.

159 "Ivy League education to the masses": Amanda Ripley, "College Is Dead. Long Live College!" *Time*, October 18, 2012.

167 "some studies have emerged": see, for example, Henry Levin and William Koski, "Administrative Approaches to Educational Productivity," in James E. Groccia and Judith E. Miller (eds.), *Enhancing Productivity: Administrative, Instructional, and Technological Strategies* (San Francisco: Jossey-Bass, 1998), 9–21.

168 Michael Cole, Peg Griffin, Kris Gutiérrez: Michael Cole and Peg Griffin: "A Socio-Historical Approach to Re-Mediation," *The Quarterly Newsletter of the Laboratory of Comparative Human Cognition* 5 (1983): 69–74; Kris Gutiérrez, et al., "Re-mediating the University:

Learning Through Sociocritical Literacies," *Pedagogies: An International Journal* (2009): 1–26.

170 "In the 1890s, 40 percent of colleges and universities": Arthur Levine, *Handbook on Undergraduate Curriculum* (San Francisco: Jossey-Bass, 1981), 57.

171 "but more rigorous research is emerging": see, for example, Clifford Adelman, "The Kiss of Death? An Alternative View of College Remediation" *National CrossTalk* (Summer 1998); Bridget Terry Long, "The Remediation Debate: Are We Serving the Needs of Underprepared College Students?" *National CrossTalk* (Fall 2005); Paul Attewell, et al., "New Evidence on College Remediation," *The Journal of Higher Education* 77 (September/October 2006): 886–924.

175 "By one count, over 50,000 have been wounded": Hannah Fischer, "U.S. Military Casualty Statistics: Operation New Dawn, Operation Iraqi Freedom, and Operation Enduring Freedom," Congressional Research Service, February 5, 2013.

188 Michael B. Katz, *The Undeserving Poor: From the War on Poverty to the War on Welfare* (New York: Pantheon Books, 1989), 7.

197 Michael Harrington. I cannot find the source for this quotation. It is in an old notebook of mine and might have come from Harrington's lecture and Q and A at the Poverty, Equality, and Justice Conference held at UCLA in September 1984.

203 "We can all agree": David Gelernter, "Misinforma-

tion Age: More Computers, Less Learning," *Weekly Standard*, January 2/9, 2006, 20–21, 21.

207   Samuel Harrison Smith, "Remarks on Education" in Frederick Rudolph, ed., *Essays on Education in the Early Republic* (Cambridge, MA, 1965), 188–189.

211   "try myself alone": quoted in Polly Welts Kaufman, *Women Teachers on the Frontier* (New Haven: Yale University Press, 1984), 19.

212   "now there are fewer than 400": Shelby Till, "One Room Schools Still Successful," http://www.360 -edu.com/commentary/one-room-schools-still -successful-.htm#.Ug2E6KXfhLI.

212   For a thoughtful treatment of the one-room schoolhouse in American cultural history, see Jonathan Zimmerman, *Small Wonder: The Little Red School House in History and Memory* (New Haven: Yale University Press, 2009).

212   Hamlin Garland, *A Son of the Middle Border* (New York: Macmillan, 1925), 95.

215   John Dewey, *Democracy and Education* (1916, New York: The Free Press, 1966), 159.

225   David Montgomery, *The Fall of the House of Labor: The Workplace, the State, and American Labor Activism, 1865–1925* (Cambridge: Cambridge University Press, 1987).

231   Howard P. Segal, *Technological Utopianism in American Culture* (Chicago: University of Chicago Press, 1985).